LONDON

A pocket guide to the city's best
cultural hangouts, shops, bars
and eateries

PENNY WATSON

Hardie Grant

TRAVEL

CONTENTS

Introduction … v
A perfect London day … vii
London overview map … viii

INTRODUCTION

London is one of the world's iconic cities, rivalling European greats like Paris and Rome for grandiose edifices and stately architecture, and New York for world-class creativity, ideas and culture. With thousands of years of history, back to when it was Londinium in Roman times, to once being the world's largest empire, it's steeped in history. It's a city where the Royal Family is still idealised and romanticised to fairytale proportions; where pomp, pageantry and ceremony attract mass crowds; where countless movies and TV series are filmed; and where celebrities – from movie stars and singers to authors and chefs – flock to live. It is a multicultural meeting point, an enriching and diverse microcosm where polyglot residents from around the globe speak more than 300 languages. But it also holds onto those loveable English traditions where tea-drinking clichés and Hugh Grant stereotypes still induce a smile.

This heady mix helps make London one of the most visited cities in the world. This fact, combined with the almost insurmountable size and scope of the city, might sound a tad intimidating, but it needn't be. To get around, you can catch the Tube (underground train network) or stay above ground and ride the iconic red double-decker buses. If you're wanting a chat, hail a fantastically old-school swish black cab. Or walk. Distances between inner-London precincts aren't huge. It's a five-minute walk between Soho's Leicester Square Tube and Covent Garden Tube stations, for example, and a 30-minute walk between Notting Hill Gate and South Kensington Tube stations.

For this guide, I've walked my favourite London streets countless times so that you can arrive and zero-in on places that resonate. My recommendations pin-down the must-do attractions, then lead you off the main streets to creative shops, bars, eateries and local hangouts in the heart of London's best precincts. And even if you've been to London before, you'll find lesser-known places and fall in love with its charm all over again. If this book takes you somewhere I've recommended, let me know (www.pennywatson.com.au; Instagram: watson_penny). If it helps you to find your own, share the love.

Penny Watson

A PERFECT LONDON DAY

My perfect days in London are many and varied. This is just one. Start central in Covent Garden at **Fabrique Artisan Bakery** where breakfast comes in the form of flaky cinnamon and cardamom buns. Stroll to **Trafalgar Square** for an obligatory photo by **Nelson's Column**. Meander back through Seven Dials to **Covent Garden Market** taking a sneak-peek at **Super Superficial** T-shirts and **Tatty Devine** jewellery bling along the way. Enjoy the festive atmosphere of the market's buskers and stalls before navigating your way to **Somerset House** to check-out the bookshop, exhibitions and architecture. Cross the **Waterloo Bridge** and enjoy the boats and the views along the River Thames as you go. On the other side, London's **South Bank** promenade is a buzzy place where you can marvel at the oak tree avenues, book market, skaters and ice-cream eating crowd before continuing south along the Thames Path to **London Eye** observation wheel. Decide to ride or save your sky-high sightseeing for later in the day. From here the **Thames Clipper** ferry (or the 25-minute Thames Path walk) will drop you downriver at the brown-brick **Tate Modern**, in the former Bankside Power Station. Enjoy contemporary art with the downloadable highlights tour then head to **Tate Modern Restaurant**, on level 9, for lunch or just enjoy the Thames' views. From up here you'll see the **Millennium Footbridge**, which is directly aligned with **St Paul's Cathedral**. If your legs are still working, cross the bridge for a closer look, otherwise continue along the river past **Shakespeare's Globe** theatre from where it's a 10-minute walk to open-air **Borough Market** – another perfect lunch spot and London's oldest market with vendors selling fresh produce and European delicacies. If you didn't go on London Eye earlier, catch panoramic views on the 72nd floor (open-air top) of **The Shard** for sunset. You can tick off most of London's icons, including nearby **Tower Bridge** and **Tower of London**. Next stop is Bermondsey High Street's **José Tapas Bar** for authentic Spanish fare and a glass of cava. Alternatively, **40 Maltby Street** does natural wine and share plates with a French spin. From here, the craft brewers along **Bermondsey Beer Mile** are your key to a late night. Alternatively, from The Shard, head back to Soho for dim sum at **Bao** or Sri Lankan at **Hoppers** and a West End theatre show.

LONDON OVERVIEW

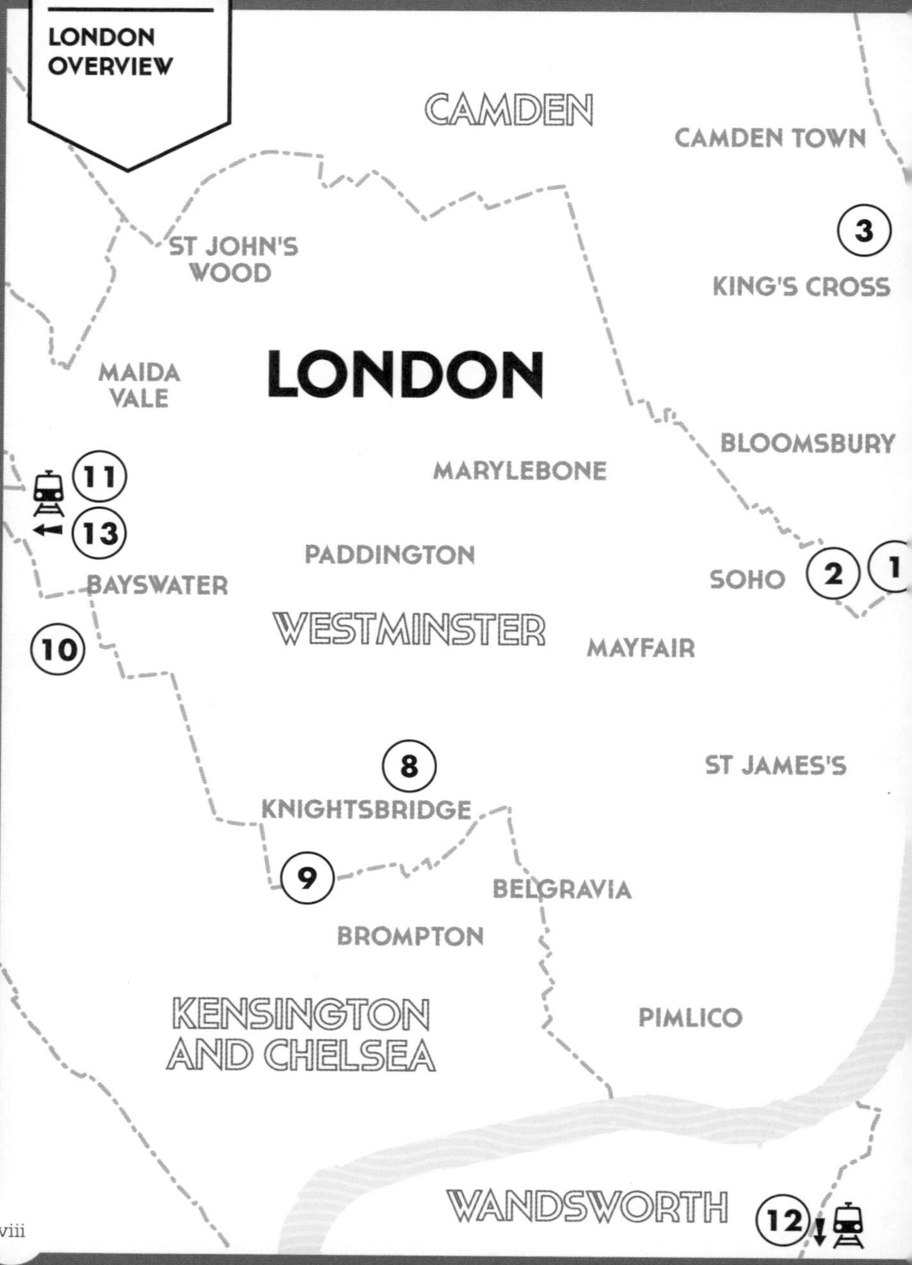
CAMDEN
CAMDEN TOWN
3
ST JOHN'S WOOD
KING'S CROSS
MAIDA VALE
LONDON
BLOOMSBURY
MARYLEBONE
11
13
PADDINGTON
SOHO
2
1
BAYSWATER
WESTMINSTER
MAYFAIR
10
8
ST JAMES'S
KNIGHTSBRIDGE
9
BELGRAVIA
BROMPTON
KENSINGTON AND CHELSEA
PIMLICO
WANDSWORTH
12

CANONBURY

ISLINGTON

HACKNEY

SHOREDITCH

RKENWELL

(4)

SPITALFIELDS

CITY OF
LONDON

(6)

SOUTH
BANK

(5)

BERMONDSEY

NEWINGTON

MBETH

UXHALL

SOUTHWARK

KENNINGTON

(14)

(7)

COVENT GARDEN

With the historic Covent Garden Market (*see* p. 2) at its centre, Covent Garden is a recreational and retail hot spot, a convenient place for friends to socialise somewhere central surrounded by the city's most evocative old-London heritage and atmospheric shopping. It's a great precinct to grab a meal before or after a theatre show in neighbouring Soho or just to idle away time exploring charming streets. All the big name local and global brands have shopfronts in the characteristic old streets and laneways around the market and Covent Garden Tube, and if you wander towards Soho, through the Seven Dials area, the offerings get more independent with some small bars, cafes and local labels still braving the big rents. On the other side of the market, towards the Thames, Somerset House (*see* p. 3) is an architectural marvel with a buzz inspired by the in-situ creative scene. You could spend all day just browsing in the bookshop.

Tube: Covent Garden, Leicester Square

→ *A changing guard stands sentry at Covent Garden Market*

1

1 COVENT GARDEN MARKET

The Market Bldg, 41, WC2E 8RF
020 7420 5856
www.coventgarden.london
Open Mon–Sat 10am–7pm,
Sun 11am–4pm
Tube Covent Garden
[MAP p. 165 F4]

Older Brits speak sentimentally about the old Covent Garden Market and the 'real Londoner' stallholders – women with cigarettes stuck to their bottom lip selling flowers and men in big coats breathing out steam as they hauled boxes of broccoli around. Today's market, which moved here in 1974, does lack some of the barter and bustle of the original (you can only imagine what it would have been like in the 18th century), but the retail hub is still eye-popping and wonderfully London with bunting and Union Jack flags. The neoclassical covered market building, in the middle of the piazza, is made up of two inner courtyards, where opera singers and knife jugglers entertain while you pop between cafes, shops, eateries and stalls. The **Apple Market** has crafty bags, jewellery and indie clothes stalls, a contrast to the heritage **Central Arcade** with its bespoke perfumes and artisan gelato shops. **Jubilee Market** is a kitsch joint selling antiques and tacky souvenirs on alternate days.

POCKET TIP
High-end international brands surround the market, alongside London Transport Museum, St Paul's Church and the Royal Opera House.

2 SOMERSET HOUSE

Somerset House, Strand,
WC2R 1LA
020 7845 4600
www.somersethouse.org.uk
Open Mon–Tues 10am–6pm,
Wed–Fri 11am–8pm, Sat–Sun
10am–6pm
Tube Covent Garden
[MAP p. 179 B1]

It's an imposing neoclassical
building, sure, but it's not until
you're in the inner courtyard
of the city's preeminent arts
hub – and surrounded by
four-storey palatial windows,
grandiose colonnaded
balconies and a flag-topped
green dome – that you get a
sense of how impressive this
place is. What's more, you can
just walk straight in off the
street – no admission fees, no
queues, no fuss. It's worth a
visit for the architectural snoop
alone, but this is home to
creatives, artists and makers.
Navigate around revolving
installations, exhibitions,
workshops, live music gigs and
talks. Spend a leisurely hour in
the **Rizzoli Bookshop**, with
its eye-catching hard covers.
If time allows, sip on a spritzer
on the terrace overlooking
the Thames or try the zero-
waste pre-theatre menu at
Skye Gyngell's restaurant,
Spring. The famed **Courtauld
Gallery**, which charges
admission, is undergoing a
two-year renovation.

POCKET TIP

In summer, the central
courtyard is alive with
dancing water fountains,
whereas in winter you'll
find an ice-skating rink.
Both are good fun.

3

3 TATTY DEVINE

44 Monmouth St, WC2H 9EP
020 7836 2685
www.tattydevine.com
Open Mon–Sat 10.30am–7pm,
Sun 11.30am–5pm
Tube Covent Garden
[MAP p.165 D2]

Independent British stores are
hard to come by in one of the
worlds' most expensive retail
precincts, so Tatty Devine,
owned by two Londoners, is a
bit of a find. The white painted
shop facade nicely frames a
showcase of happy-happy joy-
joy jewellery, so frivolous and
upbeat in colour and design it
makes you skip a little. Choose
from gorgeous glittery mirrored
rainbow necklaces, a quartet
of coloured star earrings, big
red lipped brooches and mint-
green Gin backpacks from the
classics range. Seasonal lines
have natty themes such as
London Pride and feminism.
For a real treat-to-self have a
bespoke necklace made with
your name, or your girlfriend's,
sprawled across it.

4 SUPER SUPERFICIAL

22 Earlham St, WC2H 9LN
020 7240 6116
www.supersuperficial.com
Open Mon–Sat 11am–7pm,
Sun 12pm–7pm
Tube Covent Garden
[MAP p. 164 C2]

I love a good 'T' and, when rubbed between thumb and index finger, the thick, soft quality cotton of Super Superficial T-shirts is reason enough to step into this corner local with a heritage shopfront. As well as ticking the box for comfort, these unisex T-shirts are created by artists and unique to this label. The smart designs could see them sitting comfortably in a co-working space as much as at your local. Choose from two dozen designs, from humourous stylised sketches such as Doggy – a poodle with an eccentric hair-do by Kamwei Fong – to more graphic designs like Jenga – a tower of falling blocks by Toma Vagner. The T-shirts come in black, white and contemporary shades straight from the pantone chart. Sweatshirts and hoodies are also available in the same designs and there is a small selection of sunglasses in the window. The T-shirts are discounted if you buy more than one.

5 ROCOCO CHOCOLATE**S**

38 Earlham St, WC2H 9LH
020 3887 6845
www.rococochocolates.com
Open Mon–Sat 11am–7.30pm,
Sun 12pm–6pm
Tube Covent Garden
[MAP p. 165 D2]

Roald Dahl's *Charlie and the Chocolate Factory* was the inspiration behind much of the produce in this colourful blue-shuttered shop, dedicated to all things chocolate, in Seven Dials. Its founder, Chantal Coady, has been selling artisan single-origin chocolate since 1983. Such is her dedication, she became the first to receive an OBE (Officer of the Most Excellent Order of the British Empire) for 'Services to Chocolate Making'. Proof of her passion is in the produce with a line of chocolate bars dedicated to Dahl's famed novels, such as a scrumptious peach-flavoured white chocolate bar, a la *James and the Giant Peach*. Coady's second love, design, is to thank for the exceptional packaging, which turns each little sweet-tooth offering – be it a bag of jelly beans or drinking chocolate into an exquisite gift. There's a white-glove selection of single chocolates and truffles, or try artisan chocolate bars with flavours such as orange blossom, and Persian lime.

POCKET TIP
Around the corner at 7 Mercer Street, Stanfords is an iconic travel bookshop and map emporium.

6 HOME∫LICE

13 Neal's Yard, WC2H 9DP
020 3151 7488
www.homeslicepizza.co.uk
Open Mon–Sun 12pm–11pm
Tube Covent Garden
[MAP p. 165 D1]

Tracking down Homeslice for a 20-inch wood-fired pizza has the added bonus of getting you to Neal's Yard, a leafy sunlit courtyard enclosed by lofty thin terrace houses with bottom-level shops and cafes. It's a little London surprise that reminds me of something you'd find in Amsterdam. But back to Homeslice. These guys started with a mobile pizza oven serving authentic Italian pizza to festival goers. It was so adored by the munchie crowd that the business moved into Neal's Yard and has since spawned four other eateries. Nab one of the few first-come-first served outdoor seats or settle on wooden bench seats indoors; and check the blackboard menu for out-there specialties that include a kimchi, porcini cream and basil pizza or a four-cheese, jalapeno salsa and rye crumb pizza. Buy the full 20-inch or go for just a slice and pair it with a craft beer or Aperol Spritz. There's take-away, too.

7 FABRIQUE ARTISAN BAKERY

8 Earlham St, WC2H 9RY
020 72401392
www.fabrique.co.uk
Open Mon–Fri 8am–8pm,
Sat–Sun 9.30am–6.30pm
Tube Covent Garden
[MAP p. 164 C2]

The drawcards to this artisan bakery-cum-cafe, which originated in Stockholm, are the cinnamon and cardamom buns, the glistening knots of delectable pastry lined up in sentinel rows behind the glass counter. Though it's small, it has an industrial feel with factory-sized bell lights hanging over the counter and big square white tiles reaching to high ceilings. But it's softened with blue-hued mosaic floor tiles, little vases of fresh pink carnations and pendant lights hanging intimately over a row of small antique marble-topped tables. From the wooden bench seat along one wall, seated patrons watch as (mostly) bearded Londoners file in for their morning pick-me-up – a bun in a brown bag, a pot of fresh yoghurt and a drip brew, latte or hot chocolate. At lunch time, you'll be lucky to get one of the Mediterranean-style ham and prosciutto rolls or the nut-topped brownies and icing sugared, jam-filled tarts. There's a fridge full of cloudy artisan juices and these guys are allergen friendly. Just ask.

8 THE E/CAPOLOGI/T

35 Earlham St, WC2H 9LD
020 7240 5142
www.escapologistbar.co.uk
Open Mon–Sat 5pm–12.30am,
Sun 5–11.30pm
Tube Covent Garden
[MAP p. 165 D2]

If it's cold or raining (and let's face it, that's likely in London), head down to the cosy Victorian-era innards of Escapologist, in a heavily wood-adorned vaulted basement in Seven Dials. The decor is on-theme with cut glass stemware, copper cocktail shakers, a long wooden bar and intimate leather booth seating. It's played up as a 'part modern day Victorian men's club' and 'part Masonic lodge', but the gimmickry is unnecessary because the cocktails are reason enough to visit. The rum-based 'flaming zombie' is served in a creepy white 'skull' with a flaming sugar cube, and the vodka-based 'porn-star martini' has half a passionfruit floating on a vanilla and prosecco crema. Happily, the food isn't Victorian era. Soak up the booze with pizzas, both sweet and savoury. The happy hour from 5–7pm is a good op for cheap drinks.

SOHO

With a buzz that's palpable, Soho is London's party place, its streets crowded with cool-as-funk eateries and loud bars where patrons spill onto the footpath with merry abandon. All those famous London shopping streets: Oxford, Regent, Carnaby, and squares: Leicester, Trafalgar and Piccadilly Circus, are here. A visit to London wouldn't be complete without seeing a show – or several, so head to the West End theatre district. At its heart is Shaftesbury Avenue (*see* p. 14), with its famed theatres and dazzling billboards. You'll find longstanding classics, iconic musicals and plays, as well as new ones often starring famed film and TV actors. Soho's pre- and post-theatre dining scene buzzes, and the area is also famously LGBTIQ friendly – even the letterboxes are painted in rainbow colours. Chinatown is another string to Soho's bow. You could dine at on-trend eateries Bao (*see* p. 20) or Hoppers (*see* p. 22) before seeing a show, then end the evening with a cocktail or two at Opium (*see* p. 24), one of Chinatown's best-kept secrets (until now). So, detour off Oxford and Regent streets, grab a theatre ticket (*see* p. 14), and head into Soho's backstreets.

Tube: Leicester Square, Oxford Circus, Piccadilly Circus, Charing Cross, Tottenham Court Road

→ *Britain's iconic red telephone booths can still be found in Soho's streets*

SIGHTS
1. Shaftesbury Avenue
2. National Portrait Gallery

SHOPPING
3. Carnaby Street
4. Phonica Records
5. Reign Vintage

EATING
6. Bao
7. Hoppers

DRINKING
8. The London Gin Club
9. Opium

1 SHAFTESBURY AVENUE

W1D 5ER
Tube Leicester Square
[MAP p. 164 B2]

Oversized billboards with bedazzling bulbs, neon writing touting the latest West End hits and queues of hopefuls blocking the pavement for last-minute tickets: this is Shaftesbury Avenue in the West End theatre district. It stretches from Piccadilly Circus to New Oxford Street and is one of London's most iconic destinations and a marvel to walk around even in broad daylight. The curved street, spoilt with grandiose 19th-century architecture, boasts theatres, including the **Apollo** – best for comedies, small-scale plays and light opera; the **Lyric** – the oldest theatre on Shaftesbury Avenue, opened in 1888; and the **Palace**, which opened three years later and is showing the record-breaking (9 Olivier Awards) *Harry Potter and the Cursed Child*. Another Olivier-winning new hit is young British drag queen show *Everybody's Talking About Jamie* (**Apollo**), or go for the famous longstanding classics such as *Les Misérables* (**Queens**) and *The Lion King* (**Lyceum**).

POCKET TIP
For deals on plays, musicals and shows, book online at www.londontheatre.co.uk or head to the ticket booth in Leicester Square.

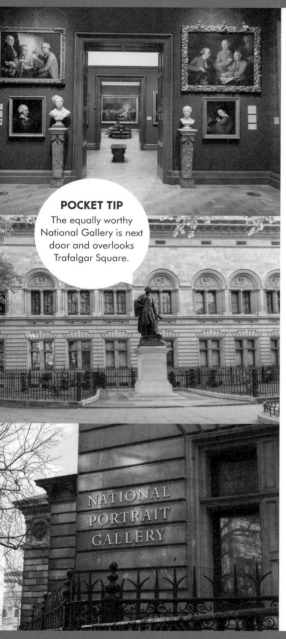

2 NATIONAL PORTRAIT GALLERY

St Martin's Place, WC2H 0HE
020 7306 0055
www.npg.org.uk
Open Sun–Thurs 10am–6pm,
Fri 10am–9pm
Tube Charing Cross
[MAP p. 169 F2]

POCKET TIP
The equally worthy National Gallery is next door and overlooks Trafalgar Square.

There's something strangely alluring about famous faces painted in portrait, be they poets, historians, lovers, fighters, kings or athletes. This contemporary gallery, in an Italian Renaissance-style building just off Trafalgar Square, has a rotating collection of 11,000 portraits spanning from the Tudors of the 16th century to present day. You can stroll in off the street, drop a donation in the box, and spend 20 minutes circling the spectacular annual BP Portrait Award exhibition, which has been on-show here for the past 40-plus years. Alternatively, spend some time immersed in historical periods – Victorian women pioneering the struggle for political representation, for example, and cultural themes like Picturing Friendship – portraits that record and affirm the bonds of friendship. Among my favourites are a portrait of Anne Boleyn by an unknown English artists in the 16th century and *Amy-Blue* a portrait of Amy Winehouse by Marlene Dumass in 2011.

3 CARNABY /TREET

W1F 9PS
Tube Piccadilly Circus, Oxford Circus
[MAP p. 166 B4]

Given its historic reputation as the epicentre of swinging '60s mini-skirted London, Carnaby Street itself is a tad underwhelming save for the arched Carnaby Street sign and big glittery Union Jack flag (which garners a lot of Instagram attention). Global fashion labels include **Scotch & Soda**, **Pepe Jeans**, **Diesel**, **True Religion**, **The Koogles**, **Sweaty Betty** and cult sassy Swedish label **Monki**. **Irregular Choice** is a standout for outrageously creative shoes adorned in a riot of colour and glitter – it's the stuff girly girls' dreams are made of. For British menswear, **Pretty Green** is Oasis' Liam Gallagher's fashion label. Head into **Liberty**, the classic department store famed for fabric, in a remarkable Tudor building with four levels of elegant wares. It has a street-level food hall where you can buy iconic Brit produce, including sloe gin and rhubarb jam. Non-edible and fun London-themed souvenirs can be found at **We Built this City**. For more boutique labels venture into surrounding Newburgh and Beak streets.

POCKET TIP
Just off Carnaby Street, find the mosaic *Spirit of Soho* mural. Watch what happens when the clock strikes on the hour.

4 PHONICA RECORDS

51 Poland St, W1F 7LZ
020 7025 6070
www.phonicarecords.com
Open Mon–Wed & Sat
11.30am–7.30pm, Thurs–Fri
11.30am–8pm, Sun 12pm–6pm
Tube Oxford Circus
[MAP p. 166 C3]

Phonica, which opened in 2003 but feels more like something out of '70s Soho, is understated but eternally cool in a muso kind of way. Fave band T-shirts and tote bags hang from the ceiling, bikes are wheeled inside with abandon and shelves are packed with CDs and endless vinyl from house, disco and techno to funk, hip hop, latin and nu jazz. There's a bar with headphones for listening to new releases and old favourites on re-release. Phonica collaborate with musicians and artists to release in-house labels (Peggy Gou's Travelling Without Arriving caught my attention) and specialise in premium handmade limited-edition releases. If you tap into the staff's encyclopedic knowledge, you could be here for hours.

5 REIGN VINTAGE

12 Berwick St, W1F 0PN
020 3417 0276
www.reignvintage.com
Open Mon–Sat 11am–8pm,
Sun 11am–7pm
Tube Oxford Circus
[MAP p. 167 D3]

Since 2009, Reign Vintage has helped fit-out Soho's boho peeps with tricked up second-hand garb that puts the awe back into wardrobe. The store, which has a view onto Berwick street food market by day, has a supplier in Italy ensuring much of the stock is endowed with labels you'll recognise; and the stock is all expertly sorted with a fashionista's eye into easily accessible genres. Flick along the hangers to find Armani jeans and Gucci T-shirts; and dig a bit deeper for gorgeous pattern-heavy '70s dresses by Pierre Cardin and check-patterned blazers by Ermenegildo Zegna (they're back in, don't you know). There are shelves dedicated to pumps, trainers and high-heels both worn-once and well-loved, and you can complete the look with an array of leather belts and handbags. Ever appreciative of global visitors, Reign will ship your bespoke Soho collection back home.

6 BAO

53 Lexington St, W1F 9AS
www.baolondon.com
Open Mon–Wed 12pm–3pm
& 5.30–10pm, Thurs
12pm–3pm & 5.30–10.30pm,
Fri–Sat 12pm–10.30pm, Sun
12pm–5pm
Tube Piccadilly Circus
[MAP p. 166 C4]

Bao is doing big things in a small space and the crowd, ever itching for something new, is loving it. In a sparklingly clean white and blonde interior, guests sit around small tables and on stools at the central three-sided counter, where they're handed a Chinese dim-sum style tick-box menu with a choice of twenty or so Taiwan-inspired dishes, including six bao. For the shamefully unenlightened, bao are the cloudlike soft, steamed buns, or baozi, that have rightfully taken the planet by storm. Bao make theirs in-house daily. The fried chicken bao with Sichuan mayo, hot sauce, golden kimchi and coriander served in a speckled sesame seed bun is bang-on for flavour. Team it with one or two xiao chi (small eats), like the aubergine and wanton crisps or scallop with yellow bean and garlic. Such is the cult of Bao that T-shirts, totes, tea-towels and worker jackets are also on the menu.

7 HOPPERS

49 Frith St, W1D 4SG
020 3319 8110
www.hopperslondon.com
Open Mon–Thurs 12pm–
2.30pm & 5.30–10.30pm,
Fri–Sat 12pm–10.30pm
Tube Leicester Square
[MAP p. 164 A2, 167 F3]

All hail Hoppers. This tiny shop with only a handful of tables is attracting patient queues of hungry patrons each night, partly because it's small but also because it's dishing out something new and exciting. The crew here has taken Sri Lankan street food from the toddy shops of home to the streets of Soho with twists on dosas, kothus, roasts and hoppers. Don't confuse the egg hoppers with the string hoppers, the former is the bowl-shaped fermented rice batter and coconut milk pancake that the restaurant is named for, the latter are noodles, and a tad plain. My favourite dish is the crispy fermented rice and lentil dosa pancakes that you fill with a choice of karis (curries), chutneys and traditional Sri Lankan pol sambol, a coconut dish. Bulk it up with 'short eats' of bone marrow roti bread, chicken wings or paneer chukka (a cheese dish) and tropical cocktails with South Asian coconut-fermented spirit arrack as your baseline.

8 THE LONDON GIN CLUB

22 Great Chapel St, W1F 8FR
020 7494 2488
www.thelondonginclub.com
Open Tues–Fri 4–11pm,
Sat 1–11pm
Tube Tottenham Court Road
[MAP p. 167 D2]

Swanky gin bars are as common as sliced lime in a gimlet, but this joint is a little different. It's in the convivial front bar of the old Star Hotel and retains its retro grunge ambience with red tiled floors, eclectic chairs, old metal signs for Navy Cut cigarettes and Good Year Tyres and a faux wood-panelled bar. The place is still run by the family who opened it in the 1930s (third generation Julie, a true Soho local, quit her job at Covent Garden Market in 2012 to take over). There are 350 unique gins in stock, including the bar's own botanical Seven Dials Gin. G&T's are served in thick rimmed, stemmed 'copa' glasses with chunks of smashed ice and quality tonic. Ask for a little dish of green olives or upsize with one of the kitchen's homemade braised beef and horseradish pies made with a dash of Damson gin and served with a little green salad. Three different gin tastings are offered here, each with a selection of five different gins. Be sure to book ahead.

9 OPIUM

15–16 Gerrard St, W1D 6JE
020 7734 7276
www.opiumchinatown.com
Open Mon–Tues 5pm–1am,
Wed 5pm–2am, Thurs–Sat
5pm–3am, Sun 5pm–12am
Tube Leicester Square
[MAP p. 164 A4]

Keep your eyes peeled for a
small plaque with 'Opium'
written on it and a jade green
door manned by a friendly
security guard; through this
door and up the stairs is
Opium, a chic oriental-styled
cocktail bar on two floors. Both
floors are lavishly decorated
with Sinophile furnishings, but
the Apothecary on the second
floor is where I like to drink.
It has a red bar with smartly
vested mixologists who devise
cocktails from spirits lined
up in old medicine bottles.
A Rose by Any Other Name
is a mix of rose tea, rose-
infused vermouth, vodka and
Champagne. It is served from a
Chinese teapot, which makes
me happy, no end. Guests can
also sit on comfy chairs in the
'Tea Parlour' for single-batch
craft teas and dim sum. The
crab and samphire dumplings
and Cantonese char siu pork
buns are hen hao (very good).

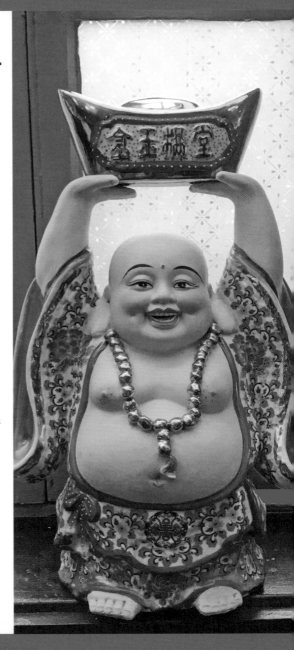

24

POCKET TIP
For more eating and drinking secrets, join Eating Europe's (www.eatingeurope.com) Twilight Soho Food Tour.

25

KING'S CROSS

Pre-2012, Kings Cross erred on the derelict side of grungy with few endearing features save for the St Pancras International terminus connecting the city with Paris via the Channel Tunnel Rail Link. But a huge swathe of industrial wasteland has since been reinvigorated and this well-connected inner-city hub is now London's it place to be. The regenerative overhaul has seen the emergence of Coal Drops Yard – an architecturally inspiring retail precinct, and Granary Square (see p. 28) – a community hub with al fresco eateries, water fountains and markets. Residents have also witnessed the renaissance of Regent's Canal (see p. 30) a meandering oasis that feels far removed from city life, and the opening of King's Boulevard, a shopping promenade that links all of the above to the station. Stylish inner-city pads (such as the fantastic canal-side Gasholders apartments, built in the old Pancras Gasworks' 1850s steel frames), shops and office hubs are popping up, and the restaurant and drinking scene is welcoming everyone with open arms. The stalwart British Library, with 200 million-plus catalogued items, has been witness to the change. If you are travelling to Europe from St Pancras International, you'd do well to add a day in King's Cross to the itinerary.

Tube: King's Cross, St Pancras, Russell Square

→ *Word on the Water book barge is a crowd favourite*

SIGHTS
1. Granary Square
2. Regent's Canal

SHOPPING
3. Canopy Market
4. Word on the Water

EATING
5. Dishoom
6. Pitted Olive

EATING & DRINKING
7. Vinoteca

DRINKING
8. The Booking Office

1 GRANARY SQUARE

1 Granary Sq, N1C 4AA
Tube King's Cross St Pancras
[MAP p.182 B1]

At King's Cross' pulsating centre is Granary Square, a public space – the same size as Trafalgar Square – with more than one thousand symmetrically placed fountains spurting choreographed water during daylight hours. It sits on a bend of **Regent's Canal** (*see* p. 30) – for centuries a smelly eye-sore and now a hive of activity – and is overlooked by the heritage Granary building, once a wheat storage and now home to famed **Central Saint Martins** fashion school (Stella McCartney and Alexander McQueen are alumni). Directly on the Square, there's **Granary Square Brasserie** and **The Lighterman** mod-Brit pub, which also has a sun umbrella-cluttered deck that overlooks the canal. Down adjoining Stable Street there are worthy eateries, including **Dishoom** (*see* p. 34) and fashion shops selling wickedly expensive sneakers. Or go the cheaper option and grab a take-away from **Benugo's** vintage Citroen coffee van and sit on the wide south-facing green-carpeted (in summer) steps that slope down to the canal.

POCKET TIP
In late 2018 neighbouring Coal Drops Yard opened: a 67-acre retail and cultural addendum with eye-candy architecture.

2 REGENT'S CANAL

Central St Martins, N1C 4AA
www.canalrivertrust.org.uk
Tube King's Cross St Pancras
[MAP p. 182 B1]

London's Regent's Canal is becoming a park-like public space that provides a leisurely sidestep of the nitty gritty city – you can walk along it, boat it, bike next to it or just sit and look at it. The canal is sandwiched between King's Cross and St Pancras International railway stations. Start from **Granary Square** (*see* p. 28) for a walk north-west along the towpath towards Camden, where horses pulling boats once plodded. You'll see **St Pancras Lock** number 4, the **Lock Keeper's cottage** and all the colourful narrow boats treading water in St Pancras basin. In the opposite direction towards Islington, you'll pass **Word on the Water** (*see* p. 32) and, on the other side of the canal after Maiden Lane Bridge, **Rotunda** restaurant, which has a terrace on the water's edge. **Battle Bridge Basin** and **London Canal Museum**, which details the history of the canal and the lives of families who lived aboard narrow boats, are next door. At **Granary Square** (*see* p. 28), green-carpeted (in summer) steps sloping down to the water are crowded with sunseekers.

POCKET TIP
You can keep walking canal-side all the way from Granary Square north-west to Camden Lock market (open daily).

3 CANOPY MARKET

West Handyside Canopy,
Granary Sq, N1C 4BH
www.kingscross.co.uk
Open Fri 12pm–8pm, Sat–Sun
11am–6pm
Tube King's Cross St Pancras
[MAP p. 182 B1]

Like everything else that's cool
in the Cross, Canopy Market
has a new hipster vibe. It's
an all-weather, year-round
weekend market normally
located under the historic
West Handyside Canopy, off
Granary Square, but in June it
goes al fresco with a summer
edition popping up at nearby
King's Boulevard. Either way,
it's a tempting little outing. It
differs from the usual farmers
and indie-style markets in that
it hasn't grown up organically.
The stalls and suppliers have
been hand-picked for a best-
of-the-best market experience
that includes the country's top
artisan food producers and a
rotating roster of designers and
artists. Stalls to look for include:
SW19London for scarves
and fashion by a duo who
graduated from nearby Central
Saint Martins; **Luminary
Baker**, a social enterprise
selling delicious cakes; and
Promises Promises for
designer Victoria Myatt's
beautiful graphic jewellery.
Arrive around Friday 5pm for
live music.

4 WORD ON THE WATER

Granary Sq, N1C 4AA
07976 886 982
Open daily 12pm–7pm
Tube King's Cross St Pancras
[MAP p. 182 B1]

This wonderfully eccentric floating bookshop, with a small stage on its roof and the sound of jazz on any given weekend, is a vision splendid. The 1920s' Dutch vessel once plied these waters, but it is now moored permanently alongside the pavement on Regent's Canal (see p. 30) at Granary Square (see p. 28). Wooed by a welcome sign, the bookish (or merely curious) can duck down inside to peruse shelves lined with affordable pre-loved and new tomes, selected by bibliophile owners Paddy Screech and Jonathan Privett. Given the enclosed space, there's not a huge selection, but you can choose from adult classics, 20th-century hard-hitters, much-loved local authors, plus a stack of childhood favourites. A little stove warms it up in winter so that there's no better spot than in that leather armchair surrounded by comfy cushions with the water lap lap lapping outside.

5 DISHOOM

5 Stable St, N1C 4AB
020 7420 9321
www.dishoom.com
Open Mon–Wed 8am–11pm,
Thurs–Fri 8am–12am, Sat
9am–12am, Sun 9am–11pm
Tube King's Cross St Pancras
[MAP p. 182 B1]

Dishoom sentimentalises the faded elegance of the once bustling old Irani cafes of India's Bombay. In an 1850s' railway transit shed, lofty metal beams, an old railway clock and Victorian brickwork are lovingly paired with mosaic tiled floors, sepia-toned photos, whirling ceiling fans and low-slung colonial furniture. The menu is similarly sentimental serving Indian fare alongside Irani cafe specialties. Start small with the likes of lamb samosas and okra fries, followed by lamb sheikh kabab and masala prawns and slow-cooked chicken berry Britannia. The house black daal, cooked for 24 hours for a thick red creamy sauce, is worth laying into one-handed with a serve of roomali roti, which comes soft, stretched and griddled straight from the hotplate. Upstairs, the dining room is jam-packed. Time your dining for a downstairs table or a seat at the bar, where mango and fennel lassi and East Indian gimlets are served by barmen in waistcoats.

6 PITTED OLIVE

3 Leigh St, WC1H 9EW
Tube King's Cross St Pancras,
Russell Square
[MAP p. 182 B4]

This authentic, family owned Turkish eatery, in a residential terraced street, doesn't advertise its phone number, has no website and is old-fashioned in the best way possible. It attracts a steady stream of locals who are greeted with a nod and a 'same as usual?' from the hard-working staff. The customers, like me, keep coming back for the Turkish gozleme, homemade in the shop window by the family matriarch. With a deft hand she pummels the little rounds of dough, flattens them on a hotplate then fills them with spinach and fetta. Take-away is cheaper, but it's worth sitting in to indulge in the accompanying salads and mezze – hummus and babaganoush dips, and burgher wheat salads. One such plate could probably feed two for lunch, or bigger appetites can head towards the rear for more tables and a choice of daily specials, such as lamb-stuffed eggplant and vegetable moussaka.

POCKET TIP
Nearby Marchmont Street, Bloomsbury, is lovely strolling territory with shops including inspiring School of Life at number 70.

7 VINOTECA

3 King's Boulevard, N1C 4BU
020 3793 7210
www.vinoteca.co.uk
Mon–Fri 7.30am–11pm,
Sat 10am–4pm & 5–11pm,
Sun 10am–4pm & 5–10pm
Tube King's Cross St Pancras
[MAP p. 182 B2]

As the name attests, this Italian restaurant and wine bar has a serious vino obsession going on. The newspaper-sized wine list, which sits at the table to be read like a weekend magazine, is 48 pages of wines that stomps around the grape-growing globe from Bordeaux and Rioja to Marlborough and Mosel. But they're not all big guns – white wines from England's Surrey and Cornwall regions get a mention, as do reds from Luxembourg and Greece. Intimidated yet? Don't be. The staff are wine savvy but informal and there's also a much smaller list with wines by the glass and (quaffable) house drops that come with an Italian menu. Try big dollops of burrata, with a skin that fissures when you cut into it, and pastas that are typically laced with capers and basil. Indoors, the decor is contemporary-industrial with lots of black metal and stressed wood with high ceilings. Outdoors, King's Boulevard provides a fine place for people-watching.

8 THE BOOKING OFFICE

St. Pancras International,
Euston Rd, NW1 2AR
www.stpancraslondon.com
020 7841 3566
Open Mon–Wed 6.30am–
12am, Thurs–Sat 6.30am–1am,
Sun 7am–12am
Tube King's Cross St Pancras
[MAP p. 182 B3]

Connecting St Pancras Renaissance Hotel with the station, this stands as one of the grandest railway station bars in Europe. If you're headed on the Eurostar, you should sneak in here. The booking office-turned champagne bar retains its Gothic Revivalist charm, with impressive arches and architraves, decorative dark wood, towering ceilings and leadlight windows. You can get comfortable in leather tub chairs with a daily newspaper and a pot of English Breakfast tea or sip Chapel Down English fizz on stools at the 29-metre bar while the waistcoated bar staff make you a swizzle-sticked Brit-themed cocktail. The snack menu includes a cured British charcuterie with piccalilli and grilled ciabatta, or head straight to dessert for Eton Mess. While the service isn't exactly five-star, the surrounds more than make up for it. Long-stayers can drop their luggage in the cloakroom.

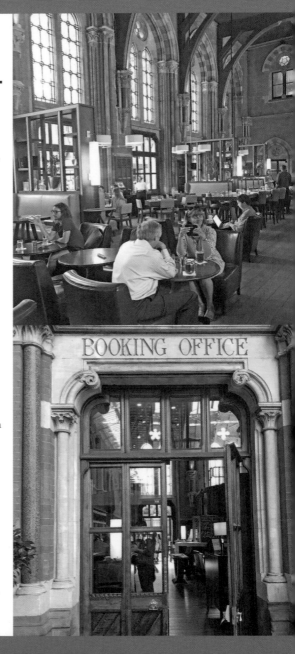

POCKET TIP

If you are/were a Harry Potter fan, there's a platform 9¾ at St Pancras – mind, you don't end up at Hogwarts.

SHOREDITCH & SPITALFIELDS

Twenty years ago, when I first lived in London, everyone was talking about a new bar that had opened in an old warehouse in Shoreditch. 'Where is Shoreditch?' was the first reaction (back then, the area was sordidly grungy, its infamous reputation as the home of Jack the Ripper still overshadowing its backstreets). The second response was, 'wow what a great idea for a big industrial room made from exposed brick'. Warehouse architecture is mainstream now and this once groundbreaking bar has been bulldozed to make way for a tower block (which tells its own story of encroaching development). But Shoreditch and its neighbour Spitalfields are palimpsest East London communities that have evolved from being on the outer edges to becoming world-beatingly exciting neighbourhoods.

There's Spitalfields Market (see p. 46), full of local makers and artists, and a crafty artisan hipster vibe going on in the surrounding streets. You'll also find that generations of different cultures have left their mark – not least in Brick Lane (see p. 42), famed for its Bangladeshi cuisine.

Tube: Liverpool Street, Old Street, Aldgate, Aldgate East

→ *Brick Lane's creative community brings the streets alive*

SAVE THE NHS
DON'T PUT PROFITS IN THE HANDS OF SHAREHOLDERS. SAVE THE

SIGHTS
1. Brick Lane

SHOPPING
2. CA4LA
3. Labour & Wait

SHOPPING & EATING
4. Boxpark
5. Spitalfields Market

EATING
6. Beigel Bake

EATING & DRINKING
7. St. John Bread and Wine
8. The English Restaurant
9. Smoking Goat

DRINKING
10. The Pride of Spitalfields

1 BRICK LANE

Brick Lane, Spitalfields, E1 6QL
Tube Aldgate East
[MAP p. 183 C3]

Brick Lane's spicy and piquant aromas, and street signs that flaunt shop names like **Cinnamon**, **Rajmahal Sweets** and **Balti House**, hint at another world. Stretching three quarters of a mile, this is one of London's most famous streets, home to successive waves of immigrants beginning with the French Huguenots in the 17th century and continuing with the Irish and Jewish communities through the 19th and 20th centuries. Today, it's the heartbeat of the Bangladeshi community, who have stamped it with the name Banglatown and turned its southern end into a default place for that adopted English mainstay meal – the curry. **Aladin**, which opened in 1971, is one of the oldest, serving vegetable Bengali curry (mind the green chillies), lamb bhajan (with 18 different spices) and chicken tikka masala (which is said to have been invented for the mild English palate). For dessert, try a jalebi street treat from **Rajmahal Sweets**.

POCKET TIP
At the overhead bridge on Brick Lane, Old Truman Brewery has music and fashion shops and Banksy's pink *Porsche* installation.

2 CA4LA

23 Pitfield St, Shoreditch,
N1 6HB
020 7490 0055
www.ca4la.com
Open Mon–Sat 11am–7pm,
Sun 12pm–6pm
Tube Old Street
[MAP p.183 A1]

'Everything in this shop is from Japan', the man behind the counter tells me matter-of-factly, 'including me'. This awesome and atmospheric hat shop first opened in Tokyo in 1997 where it pioneered the city's hat culture and industry. The London incarnation, which opened in 2006, jumped on the bandwagon of an already thriving hat scene, but there's no such thing as too many hat shops. This one has an old-fashioned shopfront and a faux antique design interior with two rooms adorned in framed butterflies, taxidermy beasts, chandeliers and dozens of old hat stands. The hats come in colours, sizes and shapes to suit any head. Try on a straw boater, bowler, soft hat, cap or beret and consider a capelin, Tyrolean or pork pie for a friend.

43

3 LABOUR & WAIT

85 Redchurch St, Shoreditch,
E2 7DJ
020 7729 6253
Open Tues–Fri 11am–6.30pm,
Sat–Sun 11am–6pm
www.labourandwait.co.uk
Tube Old Street
[MAP p. 183 C2]

Since 2000, this artisan shop
in a former London pub
has specialised in everyday
household kitchen and
garden products that are
both beautifully crafted and
functional. This utility and
quality combo is what makes
owners Rachel Wythe-Moran
and Simon Watkins, both
designers, tick. You'll find
wooden spoons, tea cosies,
feather dusters and ceramic
mugs that share the shelves
with gifting goods, including
beautiful tapestry rugs,
sommelier corkscrews and
retro lampshades. There's a
curated selection of clothing –
hand-stitched jeans and Breton
striped tops from France,
alongside enamel mugs for
your next camping trip. And
for the desk-bound aesthete:
elegant wood rulers, top-notch
HB pencils and aluminium
pencil sharpeners. If you can't
fit it all in your suitcase, these
guys also ship internationally.

POCKET TIP

Stroll the length of
Redchurch Street for
more homegrown labels
such as Folk clothing
(number 45) for men
and women.

4 BOXPARK ✓

2–10 Bethnal Green Rd,
Shoreditch, E1 6GY
www.boxpark.co.uk
Open Mon–Sat 11am–7pm,
Thurs 11am–8pm, Sun
12pm–6pm (fashion)
Mon–Sat 8am–11pm, Sun
10am–10pm (food & drink)
Tube Old Street
[MAP p. 183 B2]

It touts itself as the world's first pop-up retail mall, but happily it has popped up for good – and to me the black and white angular venue is more of a market. Made entirely from shipping containers, it started with a fashion, food, arts and lifestyle focus, with the aim to provide start-up labels and creative brands with cheap rentals. That philosophy has kind of dropped away and it has found its flow with food and fashion. There are successful brands here now, but the vibe is good, affordable shopping with plenty of one-offs and boutique buys. Check-out **Sprayground's** matching skateboards and backpacks, **Only the Blind's** embroidered silk bomber jackets and **One O Eight's** gingham loose-fit shirts and satin scarves. Upstairs, food joints such as **Felafalicious** and **Coqfighter** serve smashable pitas, burgers and craft brews in a lively beer garden that harnesses that much-coveted community vibe.

POCKET TIP
Shoreditch High Street Overground station is right next door to Boxpark.

5 SPITALFIELDS MARKET ✓

56 Brushfield St, Spitalfields,
E1 6AA
020 7375 2963
www.spitalfields.co.uk
Open Mon–Sun 10am–7pm
Tube Liverpool Street, Aldgate,
Aldgate East
[MAP p. 183 B3]

Way back in the 1660s, King Charles II granted the right to hold a market in the East End on Thursdays and Saturdays, and Spitalfields Market was born. It was in a field next to a hospital and priory known as St Mary's Spittel and grew rapidly as the area's fresh fruit and veg hub. The success of the area encouraged waves of immigrants – French Huguenot, Irish, Jewish and Bangladeshi settlers – and the market became the heartbeat of a rich and diverse polyglot community. The produce market moved out in 1991, making way for the regeneration of the market as it is today. Londoners congregate here en mass on the weekends for stalls spruiking crafty interiors, jewellery and hats, and food stalls and restaurants cooking up all sorts – from duck wraps to doughnuts. Invest in a cupcake or croissant from **Lola's Bakery** and pair it with a cold draft coffee from **Climpson & Sons**.

POCKET TIP
Sundays and Thursdays are Art Market days, with traders selling original canvasses, framed photographs and screenprints.

6 BEIGEL BAKE

159 Brick Ln, Spitalfields,
E1 6SB
020 7729 0616
Open daily 24-hours
Tube Old Street
[MAP p. 183 C2]

Prepare to queue at one of the East End's most beloved food institutions. This traditional bagel bakery, with signage like a high street chippie, is one of only two Yiddish retail businesses still remaining in Spitalfields. While the Jewish community might have moved away, Beigel Bake remains open 24-hours a day, seven days, to feed a constant turnover of late-night drinkers and clubbers, hungry hungover peeps and everyone in between. The bagels are boiled (not steamed) for about four hours, which give them a delectable crisp crust and chewy interior. Fillings include chicken, tuna and mayo, salmon and cream cheese, or, my pick, hot saltbeef, which is slathered in homemade hot English mustard and served with a side of pickled gherkin. The New York-style desserts – cheesecake, apple slice and strudel – round the munchies off nicely.

POCKET TIP
Beigel Shop, next door, was originally owned by the same family. Put the two to the beigel test yourself.

7 ST. JOHN BREAD AND WINE

94–96 Commercial St,
Spitalfields, E1 6LZ
020 7251 0848
www.stjohnrestaurant.com
Open Mon 9am–10pm, Tues–
Sat 9am–11pm, Sun 9am–10pm
Tube Liverpool Street, Aldgate,
Aldgate East
[MAP p. 183 C3]

A bacon sandwich (sarnie) is
the ultimate English high-carb,
veg-free, fat-loaded start to
the day, and I'm very partial
to them. If you're a bacon
sarnie virgin, let chef Fergus
Henderson's be your first. His
St John restaurant is all white
walls, wood floors and a bar
backed by vino bottles. His
sarnies are pretty good-looking,
too. Rashers of rare old spot pig
bacon from Gloucestershire
are stacked between home-
made doorstopper chunks of
white bread that bears a smoky
flavour from being charred on
the grill. The bread is lathered
with lashings of pure butter,
which melts to perfection
when it meets hot bacon. The
final touch is the ketchup,
made in-house with organic
tomatoes and, if my palette
serves me well, apples. Follow
it with a strawberry cream and
butterscotch doughnut or a
local Eccles cake, a traditional
treat from Lancashire with
dried fruit innards and a flaky
pastry casing.

8 THE ENGLISH RESTAURANT

50/52 Brushfield St, Spitalfields, E1 6AG
www.theenglishrestaurant.com
Open Mon–Fri 8am–11pm, Sat 9.30am–11pm, Sun 9.30am–7pm
Tube Liverpool Street, Aldgate, Aldgate East
[MAP p. 183 B3]

There was a time when England's lack of culinary prowess would have turned gourmands off this place, merely because of its name. Now, with English cuisine having been taken up a notch (or three) the tables have turned. Located across the road from Spitalfields Market, The English Restaurant is a charismatic former pub with wooden chairs, shiny draft beer taps and wood-panelled walls across two levels of snugness. The traditional British menu boasts farmhouse pork terrine with homemade piccalilli and beer-battered cod with triple-cooked chips, but if you only have one dish, don't go past the bread and butter pudding. It replaces the original stale bread recipe with a contemporary spin-off of delicate spongy brioche layered with sugar, butter, cinnamon, custard and a crackable caramelised top layer, similar to that of a crème brûlée. It's a morning, afternoon or evening treat.

9 SMOKING GOAT

64 Shoreditch High St,
Shoreditch, E1 6JJ
www.smokinggoatbar.com
Open Mon–Wed 12pm–3pm &
5.30–11pm, Thurs–Fri 12pm–
3.30pm & 5.30pm–1am, Sat
10am–4pm & 5pm–1am, Sun
10am–4pm & 5–11pm
Tube Old Street
[MAP p. 183 B2]

With a kick-arse chilli-hot twist on traditional Thai, this bar and eatery is so hot right now that it's smoking, so don't go expecting a table without a booking. The decor is all low-lit with dark bricks and black tables so close you could be sharing. It has the vibe and soundtrack of a pub, a sensation heightened by the eight craft draft beers available behind a bar lined with stools occupied most of the night. The kitchen eschews popular Thai dishes like pad Thai noodles for the more hearty fare of Northern Thailand. Dishes like smoked brisket and barbecue mutton massaman curry come to the table steaming, oily and emitting the kind of aromatic smells that make your tummy rumble. 'Spicy' means 'this will blow the top of your scull off'. So be warned when ordering the duck laab. Assuage the heat with a wine list that bounces between Slovakia, Spain and the US.

10 THE PRIDE OF ſPITALFIELDſ

3 Heneage St, Spitalfields,
E1 5LJ
020 8089 5014
Open Sun–Thurs 11am–12am,
Fri–Sat 11am–1am
Tube Aldgate East
[MAP p. 183 C3]

The Pride of Spitalfields, just off Brick Lane, is an excellent example of a British old-school public house, or free house. They're more a local hangout but an intrinsic part of the drinking scene. The beer, or ale, on tap, has seen a resurgence in stride with the craft beer movement, and is served from the same barrel from which it has been maturing (i.e. it's not gassed and needs to be pulled from the tap, so it has no bubbles and is unfiltered and unpasteurised). To the foreign palate this is often (ignorantly) translated as warm and flat. Owner Anne still lives upstairs and pulls the occasional beer in a bar that rocks red velvet upholstery, floral carpets, photo memorabilia and a brick fireplace. Choose an ale or try a traditional fermented apple cider. The menu here has 1980s' prices with £1.50 toasties and £3.50 hot saltbeef sandwiches – a cultural immersion, no less.

BERMOND/EY

With its upbeat main street, Bermondsey Street, pretty terrace houses, lively square and general bonhomie, Bermondsey is like a village. However, with the iconic Tower Bridge (*see* p. 57) in this precinct and modern skyscraper The Shard (*see* p. 56), it's very much in the centre of London. Crucially, it's the big city influences that inspire the precinct's unique foods and eateries, well-patronised pubs and bars, creative industries and artisan businesses. It's this combination that makes it one of my favourite London suburbs. Here you'll find famed Borough Market (*see* p. 58) and newcomer Maltby Street Market (*see* p. 60), both worth meandering through for fresh produce and mouth-watering artisan food.

In 2018, Bermondsey was voted London's 'Best Place to Live' by the city's *Sunday Times* newspaper. In its judging – which assessed jobs, crime rates, house prices, schools and location as well as culture and community spirit – it said the suburb epitomised the 'modern urban good life'. I concur entirely.

When navigating the streets, take note that Bermondsey Street is also referred to as Bermondsey High Street, which in British terms refers to the main street with all of the shops.

Tube: Bermondsey, London Bridge

→ *Bermondsey Street is the precinct's main thoroughfare*

SIGHTS
1. The Shard
2. Tower Bridge

SHOPPING & EATING
3. Borough Market
4. Maltby Street Market

EATING & DRINKING
5. Flour & Grape
6. José Tapas Bar
7. 40 Maltby Street

DRINKING
8. The Watch House

1 THE ∫HARD

32 London Bridge St, SE1 9SG
034 4499 7222
www.theviewfromtheshard.com
Open Mon–Sun 10am–10pm
Tube London Bridge
[MAP p. 184 A2]

Like a modern-day pyramid, its 11,000 glass panels glimmering in the fractured sunlight, The Shard is an unmissable addition to the London skyline. Designed by Renzo Piano and finished in 2013, the 95-storey, 310-metre building is Western Europe's tallest, a vertical city with offices, residences, restaurants and a viewing platform. Joe Public can ascend 244 metres in lifts, travelling up to 6-metres a second to floors 68–72 for mesmerising 360-degree vertiginous view. There's an ice-cream trolley and a Champagne bar, and on the upper-most level, which is open to the elements, a faux turf sitting area. On the 68th floor, the toilet cubicles have spectacular floor-to-ceiling views of London. Elsewhere in the building, with equally gawping views, splurge-worthy restaurants include **Aqua Shard** for Brit food and **Hutong** for northern Chinese. You can avoid The Shard entry price by enjoying an (albeit expensive) sunset cocktail at **GONG** vintage bar at the Shangri-La hotel on level 52.

2 TOWER BRIDGE

Tower Bridge Rd, SE1 2UP
020 7403 3761
www.towerbridge.org.uk
Open Mon–Sun 10am–5.30pm
(April–Sep), 9.30am–5pm
(Oct–March)
Tube Bermondsey, Tower Bridge
[MAP p. 184 C1]

POCKET TIP
Across Tower Bridge
is the infamous Tower
of London, home of
the Crown Jewels,
murderous tales and
layers of history.

Not to be confused with
the neighbouring and
underwhelming London
Bridge, Tower Bridge is one
of London's iconic sights. It
has a pair of stately decorative
towers and two gracious blue
spans that kiss the banks of the
River Thames on either side. Its
presence alongside the Tower
of London evokes London of a
bygone era. Finished in 1894,
the bascule (aka drawbridge)
design remains a highlight.
The bridge still lifts three to
four times a day for vessels
with tall masts (you'll find the
times on the website). When
the drawbridge is down,
pedestrians can walk through
its famed arches with amazing
views of the city's skyline. Or
buy tickets to see an historical
exhibition demonstrating
how the Victorian-age Engine
Room once opened using
steam-power (it now uses
electricity). There's also access
to the giddy 42-metre walkway,
which has recently had a
glass floor fitted. Seeing the
bridge lift from this angle is
a massive buzz, so time your
visit accordingly.

3 BOROUGH MARKET ✓

8 Southwark St, SE1 1TL
www.boroughmarket.org.uk
Open Mon–Thurs 10am–5pm,
Fri 10am–6pm, Sat 8am–5pm
Tube London Bridge
[MAP p. 181 F3]

Crowded around gorgeous green wrought-iron columns that cling to the bottom of the railway arches, this is London's oldest market. It was first mentioned in literature a millennium ago, and is still the purveyor of the city's fresh produce. Today, as ever, its lively traders, knowledgeable producers and gourmand visitors give it a bustling atmosphere that lifts the heart and satiates the senses. Market stalls selling fresh fruits and vegetables, meats and fish, and breads and pastries are intermingled with artisan shops filled with cheese, chocolates, fudge, oils, cereals and spices. You can come for breakfast and stay for lunch. Those without a pantry to stock can indulge in raclette cheese toasties at **Kappacasein**, Melton Mowbray pork pies at **Mrs Kings**, Coconut Fudge from **Whirld** and brownies from **Konditor & Cook**. Limited stalls operate on Mondays and Tuesdays so get there later in the week.

4 MALTBY STREET MARKET

Ropewalk, Maltby St, SE1 3PA
www.maltby.st
Open Sat 10am–5pm, Sun
11am–4pm
Tube Bermondsey
[MAP p.184 C3]

My Bermondsey friends
insist locals don't bother with
Borough Market (see p. 58)
since Maltby Street Market
opened. But they're a little bit
spoiled for choice – I say that
you should visit both markets.
Maltby Street, which opened
in 2010 as part of an Olympic
Games clean-up initiative,
is held in flag-festooned
Ropewalk, a narrow laneway
that runs along the rough-
hewed old brick railway arches
that have gone from grungy to
groove in the past decade. The
combination of archway shops
with speakeasy-style bars and
a rolling line-up of curated food
stalls gives the place a festive
atmosphere. Head to **Lassco**
for salvaged timber and
vintage homewares or **Little
Bird Gin** bar for experimental
London G&T tipples that might
include lavender or pickled
lemon. Grab a street table
near the food stalls including
Waffle On for rhubarb and
custard waffles, **Gyoza Guys**
for pork, shrimp and crab gyoza
and **Herman Ze German**
for big real fat tasty sausages.
40 Maltby Street winebar
(see p. 64) is also here.

POCKET TIP
Nearby Druid Street has
a string of independent
breweries (part of the
Bermondsey Beer Mile),
open from Wednesday
to Sunday.

5 FLOUR & GRAPE

214 Bermondsey St, SE1 3TQ
020 7407 4682
www.flourandgrape.com
Open Mon 5.30–10pm,
Tues–Sat 12pm–3.30pm
& 5.30–10pm, Sun 12pm–
3.30pm & 5.30–9.30pm
Tube Bermondsey, Tower Bridge
[MAP p. 184 B4]

Flour & Grape, a homemade
pasta and Italian wine bar,
adheres to satiating basic
Italian yearnings. Don't expect
the traditional primipatti and
secondi options. Small plates
of salumi, tomato and pesto
bruschetta and pork tenderloin
tonnato act as starters, then
there's a choice of eight pasta
varieties with paired sauces.
Slurp up a beef short-rib
ragu fettuccine, indulge in a
mussels, tomatoes and oregano
spaghetti or chow down on
asparagus, lemon and cured
egg yolk tagliatelle. Beside
each dish on the menu is a
recommended Italian vino. The
roasted pork shoulder tortelloni
with sage butter, for example,
works with a soave classico.
Exposed bricks and faux
pressed-metal ceilings add
heritage character, but the vibe
is young. Sit down to eat or pull
up a stool at the share tables
for sipping bar-style on Aperol
spritzes, watermelon Bellini's
and Bermondsey G&Ts 'til it's
time to stumble home.

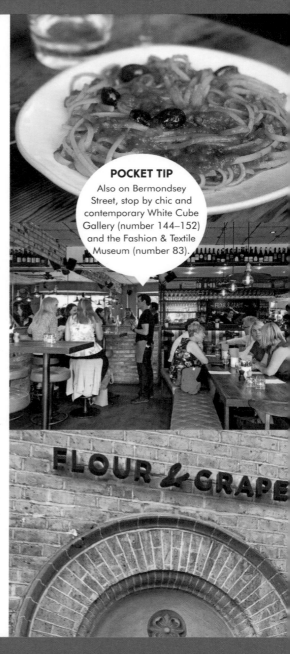

POCKET TIP
Also on Bermondsey
Street, stop by chic and
contemporary White Cube
Gallery (number 144–152)
and the Fashion & Textile
Museum (number 83).

POCKET TIP

Pizarro, the fancier sister restaurant, is one block east at 194 Bermondsey Street. It does take reservations.

BERMONDSEY

6 JOSÉ TAPAƧ BAR

104 Bermondsey St, SE1 3UB
020 7387 9455
www.josepizarro.com
Open Mon–Sat 12pm–
10.30pm, Sun 12pm–9.45pm
Tube Bermondsey, Tower Bridge
[MAP p. 184 B3]

Packed to the eyeballs with punters vying not only for barstools but for the attention of the barman, this tapas bar on a cosy corner locale on hip Bermondsey Street doesn't disappoint. It is the first love of chef José Pizarro whose expertly Andalucian dishes – dependent on the market offerings – are chalked up afresh on the blackboard daily. Regular dishes include patatas bravas (roast potatoes with a spicy tomato sauce) and pan con tomate (tomato on bread), alongside artful market specials like squid ink and octopus croquetas. The boquerones (anchovies) with green olive oil, parsley and garlic is a lesson in the simplicity of southern Spanish cuisine, as is the jamon iberico ham, a leg of which hangs tantalisingly from the squat plank ceiling. The crowd here cram around a mosaic tiled bar backed by exposed bricks and jostle for a wooden bench overlooking the high street. Bubbling cava and small glasses of beer are popular, but it's worth dipping into the sherry from Jerez. There are no reservations, so get in early.

7 40 MALTBY STREET

40 Maltby St, SE1 3PA
020 7237 9247
www.40maltbystreet.com
Open Wed–Thurs 5.30–10pm,
Fri 12.30pm–2.30pm &
5.30–10pm, Sat 11am–10pm,
Sun 12pm–5pm
Tube Bermondsey
[MAP p. 184 C3]

Light-filled 40 Maltby Street, with its shiny curved railway-arch roof, feels like a contemporary cellar door. The wine bar and kitchen, with high tables and a long bar, shares the venue with the **Gergovie Wine** warehouse which stocks wines sans chemical fertilisers and pesticides. The wine bar follows suit, pouring a dozen or so wines by the glass or bottle, with distinctive raw and natural flavours and aromas. It's not meant to bamboozle – there's a cremant d'Alsace listed under 'fizz' and a rose gamay under 'pink'. This simplicity continues in the kitchen with share plates that start at £6 for pea mousse, goats curd and oat cakes, and increases in price and portion to £15 for stewed courgettes with basil and aioli or pork ragout with fennel and crispy polenta. You could splash some cash here but stopping for a glass and plate is good value for quality quaffing.

POCKET TIP

Take your KeepCup to the neighbouring graveyard, now a small park with benches and greenery perfect for lazing with a coffee and pastry.

8 THE WATCH HOUSE

199 Bermondsey St, SE1 3UW
020 7407 6431
www.thewatchhouse.com
Open Mon–Fri 7am–6pm,
Sat–Sun 8am–6pm
Tube Bermondsey, Tower Bridge
[MAP p. 184 B4]

Measuring only a few metres in each direction, this characteristic 19th-century building was once a shelter for men guarding St Mary Magdalane Church graveyard at night. Things have sure changed. Now it looks after the caffeine scene with a steady flow of latte lovers lining up for their daily imbibe. The sound of grinding beans and hissing steam teamed with lively staff make the bustle here as addictive as the caffeine. Bags of coffee and accoutrements line the curved bricked lime-washed interior walls and, with space at a premium, the counter is jam-packed with ham and cheese croissants, pastries, chocolate brownies and banana breads. There's a wrought-iron fire inside in winter, and in summer you can settle into a flat white outside along the pavement.

ƎOUTH BANK

With the River Thames Path promenade along its entirety, the South Bank has become a destination in itself. Start at Westminster Bridge and don't forget to look back at the view of Big Ben and the Houses of Parliament. Then meander along the riverside's tree-lined path, through public spaces and sitting areas, and under the characteristic old bridges that connect it to the north bank. Along with big names like the London Eye (*see* p. 68), the British Film Institute (BFI), National Theatre, Tate Modern (*see* p. 71) and Shakespeare's Globe (*see* p. 70) (in that order), you'll pass plenty of smaller offerings where the inquisitive can find shops, bars, restaurants and galleries or just excellent viewpoints. In summer, the stretch under Waterloo Bridge fires up with buskers, food vans and entertainment, while at the other end, near London Bridge, you can watch Wimbledon on the big screen while sipping Pimms from al fresco pop-up bars. In the streets behind the riverside there's plenty to find too. A detour into The Cut is a slice of local London with the bustle of everyday life. So too, the nearby precinct of Bermondsey (*see* p. 54).

Tube: Waterloo, Blackfriars, Southwark, London Bridge, Lambeth North

→ *The River Thames' banks are home to the Houses of Parliament and London Eye*

SIGHTS
1. London Eye
2. Shakespeare's Globe
3. Tate Modern

EATING
4. Wahaca
5. Meson don Felipe

DRINKING
6. Dandelyan
7. The Travel Cafe

1 LONDON EYE

Riverside Building, County Hall,
Westminster Bridge Rd, SE1 7PB
087 0990 8881
www.londoneye.com
Open Mon–Sun 10am/11am–
6pm/8.30pm; varying hours,
check website
Tube Waterloo
[MAP p. 179 B3]

When the London Eye
observation wheel was being
built, I had a job nearby
and would spend my lunch
hour watching them piece
it together like a big puzzle.
At 135 metres (443 feet) tall
with a diameter of 120 metres
(394 feet) and its position right
next to the River Thames, it's
one of the more impressive
of the mega wheels in cities
globally. In peak times, the area
below the wheel is jammed
with queues, but it's the most
popular paid tourist attraction
in Britain for a reason. From
the big Perspex bubble in the
sky (that's what it feels like),
you can look across to St Paul's
Cathedral, Big Ben and the
Houses of Parliament, and
follow the mapping of the
Thames way up past The
Shard (see p. 56) towards
Greenwich (see p. 150). If
you chance upon a clear
blue-sky day, it's a magical
experience. For a little extra
money, it's worth buying the
fast-track option online rather
than spending your precious
holiday time in a queue.

POCKET TIP
Under Waterloo Bridge
is a second-hand and
antique book market,
open daily. Browse
as you watch river life
pass by.

SOUTH BANK

2 ƧHAKESPEARE'Ƨ GLOBE

21 New Globe Walk, Bankside,
SE1 9DT
020 7902 1400
www.shakespearesglobe.com
Open daily 10am–6pm
(box office)
Tube London Bridge
[MAP p. 181 D2]

There's nothing left of
Shakespeare's original
playhouse, which was
designed in 1599 and built
nearby, but this faithfully
reconstructed version takes
its design cues from historical
printed panoramas, written
accounts, sketches and
suggestions within the plays
themselves. The huge circular
open-air building with old-
fashioned white lime-wash
walls, hefty oak beams and a
red thatch roof has a stage that
juts out into the audience and
three tiers of balcony seating.
Seeing a play here is a unique
and memorable experience.
In days of yore, the standing
room at the bottom was for the
peasants. Today, standing room
is still the cheapest option,
just mind it's not a production
of *Hamlet* as, at 29,551 words,
it'll be a long night. There is
a summer and winter season
program but guided tours run
all year round. Keep an eye on
the Globe's Twitter feed for
last-minute standing tickets
for only £5.

POCKET TIP

In front of the Tate, the Millennium Footbridge crosses the Thames and is aligned for admiring the southern facade of St Paul's Cathedral.

3 TATE MODERN

Bankside, SE1 9TG
020 7887 8888
www.tate.org.uk
Open Sun–Thurs 10am–8pm,
Fri–Sat 10am–10pm
Tube London Bridge
[MAP p. 180 C2]

With it brown bricks and angular smoke stack, the Tate Modern is a brazen architectural landmark along the Thames. Born from the redundant Bankside Power Station in 2000, its behemoth Turbine Hall reaches 35-metres-high and stretches 152-metres-wide, and houses installations and performances that match its magnitude. The six-storey Boiler House and newer 10-storey Blavatnik Building are home to world-class artworks in industrial-sized spaces. Eye-off Dadaist Marcel Duchamp's urinal installation and Henri Matisse's colourful snail collage in the permanent collection, then have lunch on level 10 overlooking the Thames. Tate Modern is not only free, it's accessible and navigable with handy pamphlets and wall maps. Get savvy pre-visit with the free downloadable highlights tour. The brilliant bookshop has an enviable range of art, design, architecture, photography and children's books, as well as London- and art-themed gifts.

4 WAHACA

Queen Elizabeth Hall,
Southbank Centre,
Belvedere Rd, SE1 8XX
020 7928 1876
www.wahaca.co.uk
Open Mon–Sat 12pm–11pm,
Sun 12pm–10.30pm
Tube Waterloo
[MAP p. 179 B2]

Once upon a time Mexican food as we now know it didn't exist in London. Then this authentic street kitchen opened, and Brits finally cottoned on to the culinary magic of mixing lime juice, coriander and ripe Hass avocados together (guacamole for those still catching up). Since then, Wahaca has gone mainstream and opened around the country, but it maintains its big sassy personality and quality food. The South Bank venue is one of the more fun outlets, built from eight shipping containers on two levels overlooking the Thames. The bottom level, with a food truck and three colourful tables, has an abridged menu, ideal for a quick bite as you walk along the river. Slow-cooked, marinated pork burritos are topped with black beans, slaw, zingy red onion relish and habanero chillies (if you fancy them) and corn chips come smothered in guacamole. Sit under the umbrellas and watch the world walk by.

POCKET TIP
The nearby undercroft of the Southbank Centre is a graffiti-adorned skatepark that has been around for more than 40 years.

CHI.LL.I. /PPR

MASA. FLR

TACO.

A.VO. CADO

350,000 SHU
9/10

36.801 KG
86.161 LBS
9000
5.73"

571

wahaca

wahaca's
MEXICAN STREET KITCHEN

5 MESON DON FELIPE

53 The Cut, SE1 8LF
020 7928 3237
www.mesondonfelipe.co.uk
Open Mon–Sat 12pm–11pm
Tube Southwark
[MAP p. 180 A4]

In an old Midland Bank building, with bars still on the windows, this authentic 30-year-old Spanish eatery has oodles of Andalucian character and not an ounce of pretence. Sit at a big central wooden counter or at a little side table and you'll be surrounded by bullfighting sketches, painted Spanish plates, old Tío Pepe sherry bottles and walls the colour of roasted red peppers. The food is simple, traditional and delicious: plates of boquerones (anchovies) sprinkled with parsley; stuffed mushrooms served on terracotta plates; big bowls of olives drowning in chilli; and octopus marinated in olive oil and paprika. By day, paella is served to office workers from a big pan on the footpath outside, and by night flamenco guitarists serenade guests. Wines come from across Spain – Rioja, La Mancha, Alicante – and are available by glass and carafe.

POCKET TIP

The red pillars in the water near Blackfriars Bridge formed part of a railway bridge from 1864, the bridge was removed in 1985.

6 DANDELYAN

20 Upper Ground, SE19DP
020 3747 1063
www.dandelyanbar.com
Open Mon–Wed 4pm–1am,
Thurs–Sat 12pm–2am, Sun
12pm–12.30am.
Tube Blackfriars
[MAP p. 180 B2]

With only pedestrian traffic and the occasional cyclist between you and the Thames, there's nowhere closer to the water than the swanky Sea Containers London hotel's award-winning bar that is doing for cocktails what Noma in Copenhagen did for food. It's flashy, sure, and the crowd is good-looking, but you'll get a smile at the door whoever you are. Settle into blue and green velvet and leather banquettes, next to shiny metallic squat tables and cushioned poufs and note the green marble bar. It's not just drinks that are on offer here, it's an experience. The mixologists are all about molecular gastronomy with an emphasis on botanicals and fruit. By way of example, my preferred libation is the Pantone Spritz, a Plymouth gin, cocchi rosa and bubbles drink that arrives with a little shiny dollop of black rice and coriander delicately balanced on rice paper atop the glass. You fold the little parcel up and eat it, the Asian flavours perfectly enhancing the ice-laden beverage.

7 THE TRAVEL CAFE

139 Westminster Bridge Rd,
SW1 7HR
www.travel.cafe
Open Mon–Fri 8.30am–4pm,
Sat 9am–2pm
Tube Lambeth North
[MAP p. 179 C4]

A whimsical cafe-cum-shop
that will tempt you away from
the riverside and into the
village vibe of Lower Marsh.
The squeal of train wheels,
a constant around Waterloo
station, is dimmed somewhat
by the background piano
music and the hiss of the
coffee machine. This place
dabbles in a curated selection
of giftable goods – tins of
shortbread, boxes of tea and
an array, as per current decor
trend, of teeny potted cacti and
succulents. But the main aim
is drinks in the form of fresh
ground barista coffee from
London's popular Monmouth
suppliers, green tea lattes and
tea in cherry, blood orange and
berry flavours. The charmer
of an interior – white walls,
tree trunk columns and timber
floors matched with eclectic
mid-century chairs and cleverly
devised divider shelving –
keeps dulcet toned clientele
happily sipping away all
afternoon. The small selection
of London travel books
helps too.

NOMADIC
GARDEN

STAY CLOSE
TO PLANTS
THAT FEEL LIKE
SUNLIGHT

THE TRAVEL CAFE

CARTWRIGHT & BUTLER
YORKSHIRE
ENGLAND
EST. 1985

EXQUISITE
BISCUITS

Net Weight 200g℮

CARTWRIGHT & BU
YORKSHIRE
ENGLAND
EST. 1985

EXQUISITE
BISCUITS

Net Weight 200g℮

77

BRIXTON

Brixton forms SW9 (south-west 9), one of
London's oldest postcodes. It has a grungy
cool vibe that attracts musos and party people
keen on a sing-along, a dance-athon, a late
night or all three. Brixton also has a surfeit of
historical and contemporary anecdotes about
the African diaspora music, art, markets,
poets, radicals and preachers that have made
it what it is today. There's no better way to
get a sense of it than to walk the streets.
Brixton Village & Market Row (see p. 86)
and Electric Avenue (see p. 82) are eye-
candy of market stalls selling Caribbean
and African produce and eateries serving
Etrian and Jamaican food. Blaring reggae
music and street art-covered railway arches
add to the atmosphere. Pop Brixton (see
p. 87) brings modern street-eats and DJ sets
to the party, but the old institutes – the Ritzy
Picturehouse (see p. 81) and Brixton Academy
(see p. 80) – still hold their own. This is
one pocket of London that stands alone for
sheer personality.

Tube: Brixton

→ *Street art gives a big nod to Brixton's African
diaspora community*

1 BRIXTON ACADEMY (O₂ ACADEMY)

211 Stockwell Rd, SW9 9SL
020 7771 3000
www.academymusicgroup.com
Open 11am–5pm (box office)
Tube Brixton
[MAP p. 185 A1]

It has been officially called O₂ Academy since 2004, but for most of us it remains Brixton Academy, a die-hard venue where some of the world's best music acts have let loose. It started life as a cinema in 1929 and retains the Art Deco facade, but its iconic status ignited in the early '80s when it opened as a music venue. Legends abound: Eric Clapton and Dire Straits rehearsed here, Wham used the venue to shoot 'Wake Me Up Before you Go Go' and The Smiths played their final show here. Madonna, Iron Maiden, The Clash, The Prodigy, Arcade Fire, Moby, Groove Armada, the list goes on. With a sloping theatre floor, stalls, Italian Renaissance auditorium, proscenium arch stage and capacity for almost 5000 sitting and standing patrons, it retains its reputation as a formidable gig venue. Catch live music and comedy, as well as some serious club nights. Plan ahead and book early as big ticket events are sold-out almost at time of release.

POCKET TIP
Nearby Brixton Jamm is another late-night clubbing mainstay with DJ sets until 5am.

Thur 30th Aug
Death Grips

Sat 1st Sep
Nepathya - Celebrating 25 years of Nepathya

Tue 4th Sep
Ezra Furman

Thur 6th Sep
Fri 7th Sep
Incubus

Sat 8th Sep • 4pm
AFROPUNK Takeover Brixton: August Greene

Fri 14th Sep SOLD OUT
Sat 15th Sep
Garbage

Tue 18th Sep
A F#cked Up Evening With The Trailer Park Boys

Thur 20th Sep SOLD OUT
Fri 21st Sep SOLD OUT
Sat 22nd Sep
Tash Sultana

My Life Story

Thur 4th Oct SOLD OUT
Fri 5th Oct
Vulfpeck

Sun 7th Oct
Burna Boy

Tue 16th Oct
Tom Grennan

Wed 17th Oct SOLD OUT
Thur 18th Oct SOLD OUT
Jorja Smith

Sat 24th Oct
Editors

Sat 27th Oct • 9pm
Playaz Halloween

Mon 29th Oct SOLD OUT
5 Seconds of Summer

Tue 30th Oct
John Grant

Wed 31st Oct SOLD OUT
Thur 1st Nov
First Aid Kit

Tue 13th Nov
Within Temptation

Wed 14th Nov
Courtney Barnett

Thur 15th Nov SOLD OUT
Fri 16th Nov SOLD OUT
Tom Misch

Sat 17th Nov SOLD OUT
Sun 18th Nov
Leon Bridges

Mon 19th Nov
Lil Dicky

Wed 21st Nov
YUNG LEAN (Wings of Desire)

Thur 22nd Nov SOLD OUT
Fri 23rd Nov SOLD OUT
Anne-Marie

Sat 24th Nov
Honne

Sun 25th Nov
EDEN

Fri 30th Nov SOLD OUT
You Me At Six

Thur 13th Dec
Blossoms

Fri 14th Dec
Sasha Re-fract

Sat 15th Dec
Brainfeeder X

Fri 21st Dec
Clutch

Sat 12th Jan 2019
Enter Shikari

Wed 16th Jan 2019
Thur 17th Jan 2019
Fri 18th Jan 2019
Ben Howard

Thur 24th Jan 2019
ODESZA

Sat 2nd Feb 2019 SOLD OUT
Sun 3rd Feb 2019 SOLD O
Tue 5th Feb 2019
Wed 6th Feb 2019
Thur 7th Feb 2019
The Streets

Sat 23rd Feb 2019 • 8pm
Trixie Mattel - Skinny Legend Tour

POCKET TIP

The Upstairs Bar at Ritzy Picturehouse is one of Brixton's most-loved venues, featuring live music every night. Settle in for reggae, afro-beat, jazz, folk, DJ sets and blues nights.

2 RITZY PICTUREHOUSE

Coldharbour Ln, SW2 1JG
0871 902 5747
www.picturehouses.com
Open Mon–Sun 9am–8.30pm
Tube Brixton
[MAP p. 185 A3]

Old black-and-white shots of Hollywood stars grace the sides of the red-brick Ritzy Picturehouse, which was one of the country's first purpose-built cinemas when it opened in 1911 amid Brixton's booming nightlife scene. It has changed hands a few times over the century, and it's more mainstream than it was in the 1980s when it had a reputation for only showing artsy left-wing and gay films, but it still rallies for causes dear to the hearts of progressives. All five cinemas are wheelchair accessible, many of the films are audio described and/or sub-titled, autism awareness screenings take place monthly and kitchen and kiosk menus are available in Braille. The downstairs cafe is busy with latte-drinkers and popcorn-munching mainstream and arthouse matinee goers and there's a kitchen serving reasonably priced Greek-style souvlakis and snack food. **Ritzy bar**, adjoining it, has tables and an outdoor area, and a range of house red and whites and tap beers for sipping while you watch.

3 ELECTRIC AVENUE

**Electric Avenue, SW9 8JY
Tube Brixton
[MAP p. 185 B3]**

To really give Brixton's iconic market street Electric Avenue its dues, walk it Travolta-style with a cashmere coat, knee-high leather boots and some serious gold on your fingers. That was the vibe of the place in the '70s and '80s when, after the 1981 riots, Eddy Grant was inspired to write the 1980s' eponymous funk hit *We gonna rock down to Electric Avenue*. You'd be hard-pressed to find this garb these days, but the avenue – one of the first streets in London to have electricity – retains its intrigue as the authentic heartbeat of Brixton's African diaspora. The street begins just around the corner from Brixton station with a big showy sign and curves north-east with a lovely row of three-storey terraces topped by red brick chimneys built in the 1880s. On street level, the shops are indicative of the culturally eclectic neighbourhood with African beauty salons, halal butcheries, cheap electrical stores and Jamaican grocery stores. Brixton market runs along the middle, selling Bob Marley T-shirts, African mumu dresses and necklaces and factory outlet shoes.

4 THE KEEP BOUTIQUE

32/33 Brixton Village,
Coldharbour Ln, SW9 8PR
020 7924 0867
www.thekeepboutique.com
Open Mon–Sun 11am–6pm,
Sat 10.30am–6pm
Tube Brixton
[MAP p. 185 B3]

Organic, ethical, sustainable and mindful are often greenwash words, but step foot into this double-fronted boutique in Brixton Village to see real heart and soul behind the ethos. Frustrated by poor quality clothing and uninspiring shopping, Kate Richards went on a mission to find clothing and accessories that had an ethical profile. The Keep Boutique – quality clothes you can keep forever – was born in 2012. With a pretty red bicycle out the front and botanica painted windows, the shop is a pleasurable place to browse. There are soft leather bags, shorts, skirts and tops hung from racks made from tree branches, along with shoes, jewellery and candles on shelves made from recycled timbers. The men's selection is particularly cool with chunky knit jumpers, woollen scarves and organic cotton tees and shorts. Brands such as MOA, Gung-Ho and Colcha Clothing have neat little eco back stories.

5 UNITED80 BRIXTON

Brixton Village, Coldharbour Ln, SW9 8PS
www.united80brixton.com
Open Thurs–Sat 10.30am–6pm, Sun–Mon 12pm–5pm
Tube Brixton
[MAP p. 185 B3]

This funky concept store with a sleek-lined grey and yellow facade could be called 'wearable Brixton'. It is stocked by co-owner Samantha-Jane Ofoegbu, with a collection of independent emerging brands that cut through the local music, art, fashion and design scene. Many of the brands are locally made and all of them care about promoting London's African diasporan experience. Cut-on-the-cross bomber jackets and 'Black Music' sweaters join 'Art Saved My Life' T-shirts and screen-printed jumbo vests on the racks. The shelves are exactingly laid out with beard oils, badges, cards, cups and pledge pins alongside limited edition trainers and camo backpacks. The paintings and framed art might not fit into your suitcase but the pendant brass necklaces made by self-taught jeweller Susan O certainly will. She makes earrings too!

85

6 BRIXTON VILLAGE & MARKET ROW

Coldharbour Ln, SW9 8PS,
www.brixtonmarket.net
Open Mon 8am–6pm,
Tues–Sun 8am–11.30pm
Tube Brixton
[MAP p. 185 B3 & 185 C3]

Even on an overcast day this neighbourly market in interconnected arcades has a buzzy vibe. It might be the rays of light streaming through the high arched glass ceilings but it's also the neighbourhood conviviality. The stalls and shops combine old school traders – Latin and Caribbean grocers selling plantains and taro; fishmongers and stalls selling African handicrafts, wigs and domestic products. Then there's the new-school – **Lion Vibes** is a vinyl shop specialising in reggae, **Hunky Dory** does vintage garb and **Circus** has colourful leather slip-on shoes, scarves and hessian bags. The **Keep Boutique** (see p. 84) sells only sustainable clothes and designs while **United80 Brixton** (see p. 85) has handpicked prints, clothes, art and crafts with a distinctly Brixton influence. The food offerings are global. You can eat Ethiopian and Etrian vegetarian at **Hanesha Village**, Beijing dumplings at **Mamalan** or okonomiyaki (Japanese pancakes) at **Okan**.

7 POP BRIXTON

49 Brixton Station Rd, Brixton,
SW9 8PQ
www.popbrixton.org
Open Mon–Wed 9am–11pm,
Thurs–Sat 9am–12am, Sun
9am–11pm
Tube Brixton
[MAP p. 185 B2]

POCKET TIP
It's worth looking online
for upcoming events – this
place has you covered with
yoga and tai chi classes,
pop-up art and craft
workshops, vinyl parties
and DJ sets.

I love it when a shipping container gets put to good use, so when about 20 of them are bricked together like Lego to form a collective of cool in an otherwise disused space, I'm all over it. On paper, Pop Brixton is a community initiative to showcase independent businesses from Lambeth and Brixton. The reality is a kick-arse urban hive that brings together the likes of cute little tailor-cum-clothes shop **Make Do and Mend**, **Prohibition Ink** tattoo studio, **Kataba**, a teeny shop making beautifully artisan Japanese knives and **Container Records Store**. Sidelining these hipster haunts is a veritable festival of food. Tuck into global sausages at **World of Wurst**, pizza at **Made of Dough**, authentic Mexican streetfood at **Maria Sabina** and Sicilian small plates at **Franzina Trattoria**. On Friday, Saturday and Bank Holiday Sundays from 6pm, it becomes an over-18 venue, so expect tunes and tipsiness.

8 PARISSI

76 Atlantic Rd, SW9 8PX
020 7924 9022
www.parissi.co.uk
Open Mon 8am–3.50pm,
Wed–Fri 8am–3.50pm,
Sat–Sun 9am–6.30pm
Tube Brixton
[MAP p. 185 C4]

Exposed bricks, Singer sewing machine tables and dangling vines add to the character of this inspired cafe, a hub for laptop- and sketchbook-toting Brixton locals who love Greek expat owner Spyros' excellent food. Steal one of the church pew seats for a vegie stacked frittata or toasted sourdough sandwich, or head outside to a simple courtyard with sun umbrellas for something from the all-day breakfast menu: shashuka eggs or French toast with bacon and blueberries. Baked muffins and cakes come straight from the oven filling the place with sugary aromas, along with baklava and carrot cake that sits temptingly on the front counter. Fresh summery brunch cocktails include a Prosecco and gin-based elderflower fizz, or knock the top off a Brixton brew made in one of the archway breweries nearby. It's all upbeat acoustic tunes and soulful people here. Expect fresh good-quality food, a sociable drink and the hum of contentment.

contains, wheat, egg, dairy £3.10

LEMON + PISTACHIO gluten free £3

KNIGHT/BRIDGE & /T JAME/

Home to century-old gardens and impossibly beautiful Victorian edifices, Knightsbridge is unflappably affluent and as posh as can be, which makes it rather alluring. Imagine yourself being chauffeured around in a Bentley, exiting exclusive department store Harrods (*see* p. 97) with arms full of bags, before dining at a five-star velvet-roped restaurant, and you'll have some idea of how the locals live.

Sitting handsomely next door to Knightsbridge, St James is equally affluent (perhaps more-so), boasting big-hitters including royal residences Buckingham Palace (*see* p. 92) and St James Palace; famous Monopoly board streets Park Lane, Piccadilly and Pall Mall; and The Ritz London hotel.

The back streets of both Knightsbridge and St James are dreamlike to walk around with leafy trees, lovable gastro pubs and swanky shops made for a millionaire clientele. Both precincts enjoy lung-filling green spaces. Hyde Park (*see* p. 94) is on the northern boundary of Knightsbridge, including Serpentine Gallery (*see* p. 95). Green Park, which links with Hyde Park on the east and St James' Park on the west provides similar activities in a more landscaped setting. (It's a lovely walk east-west through all three if time allows).

Tube: Knightsbridge, South Kensington, Hyde Park Corner, St James's Park, Green Park

→ *The afternoon tea at Egerton House Hotel is one of London's finest*

1 BUCKINGHAM PALACE

Westminster, SW1A 1AA
030 3123 7300
www.royal.uk
Open 9.30am–7pm Jul–Aug,
9.30am–6pm Sept, Oct–June
check website.
Tube St James's Park, Hyde Park
Corner, Green Park
[MAP p. 171 F2]

Royal waves from the balcony fronting this neoclassical palace – the Queen's official London residence and a working royal palace – have either been in times of great mourning (after Lady Diana's death) or great celebration (after Prince William and Kate Middleton's wedding). Memories and newsreels of these events have helped sear the building and its residents into popular consciousness even in far-away countries. It is an essential tick box for a London visit. Book tickets to explore the 17 State Rooms, including the gold 'white drawing room', the throne room with its pink Chairs of Estate, which were used in the coronation ceremony of The Queen and The Duke of Edinburgh in 1953, and the grandiose ballroom used for State banquets. You can also book a private tour that includes garden highlights.

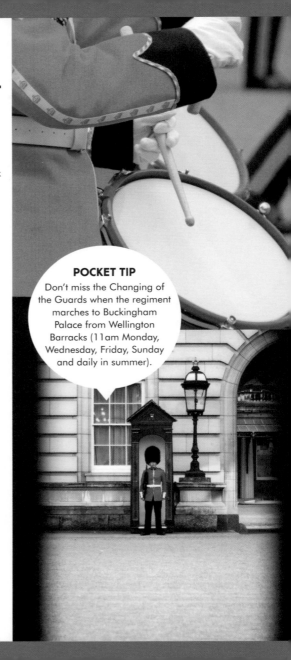

POCKET TIP
Don't miss the Changing of the Guards when the regiment marches to Buckingham Palace from Wellington Barracks (11am Monday, Wednesday, Friday, Sunday and daily in summer).

POCKET TIP

Nearby, visit Churchill War Rooms, the evocative underground nerve centre from which the prime minister and his inner circle directed World War II.

2 HYDE PARK

Knightsbridge, SW7 1SE
Tube Knightsbridge, Hyde
Park Corner, Lancaster Gate,
Queensway
[MAP p. 170 B1, 178]

Hyde Park is the largest of London's Royal Parks, a green lung covering 350 acres. It was used by Henry VIII as a private hunting ground in the 1500s, but these days it's a people's paradise. When the sun shines, glorious oaks and grassy meadows are a beacon for picnic-makers, strollers, runners, cyclists, horse riders and skaters. Visitors can row boats and swim in designated parts of the sprawling **Serpentine Lake** (accompanied by ducks and swans), and learn to ice-skate in winter. There are outdoor tables at the **Lido** cafe or hire a recliner and sit on the bank. The **Serpentine Gallery** (*see* p. 95) is among many intriguing buildings and monuments, so too the **Diana Memorial Fountain**, which kids rollick in during summer. On Sundays, head to **Speaker's Corner**, once the site of public executions, now a place for London's most vocal orators to get on their soapbox. Hyde Park connects with **Kensington Gardens**, which is home to **Kensington Palace** (*see* p. 106).

POCKET TIP

For views of Hyde Park, head to The Wellington Arch at Hyde Park Corner. You'll also find the Australian and New Zealand war memorials here.

3 SERPENTINE GALLERY

Kensington Gardens, W2 3XA
020 7402 6075
www.serpentinegalleries.org
Open Mon–Sun 10am–6pm
Tube Knightsbridge
[MAP p. 175 F2]

This small, internationally recognised gallery occupying a Grade II listed former tea pavilion (where Hyde Park becomes Kensington Gardens) is dedicated to finding innovative ways to encourage third-graders, grannies and everyone in between to engage with modern and contemporary art, architecture and design. It succeeds because it is free, has only one interior exhibition at a time and the space is easily navigated. It's also interactive. On my last visit, a project by Christo and Jeanne-Claude called *Barrels and the Mastaba 1958–2018* saw an oversized pyramid of colourful oil barrels erected on the Serpentine Lake. Its big hulk and apparent randomness were a talking point for people punting on the water or taking a walk. The gallery amps up in summer (like everything in London) with the construction of a brand-new pavilion, which is commissioned by a new architect each year. A pop-up cafe inside ensures visitors can admire it inside and out.

POCKET TIP

From Knightsbridge, neighbouring South Kensington is an easy walk. From St James, you can walk north into Soho.

4 CATH KID/TON ✓

178–180 Piccadilly, W1J 9ER
020 7499 9895
www.cathkidston.com
Open Mon–Sat 10am–8pm,
Sun 12pm–6pm
Tube Green Park
[MAP p.168 A3]

Polka dotted aprons, rosy
wallpaper, flowery ironing
board covers – Cath Kidston
started making practical and
pretty designs from vintage
fabrics back in 1993 in her
small West London shop. These
days her signature nostalgic
motifs, including strawberries,
sausage dogs, aeroplanes and
the iconic Brampton Rose,
have gone global and are now
so emblematically English they
make great souvenirs. If you
only visit one store, make it
this flagship shop on Piccadilly
where the nostalgia lives on in
the cheerily playful decor and
stock including everything
from pyjamas and bedsocks
to make-up bags and totes.
The London icon range of
plates, umbrellas, KeepCups
and more, has a retro design
featuring Buckingham Palace
and the Changing of the
Guards – a fitting purchase
in this part of town.

POCKET TIP

Next door, Fortnum and
Mason department store
encapsulates a different
England – one of refined
elegance. Buy chocolates,
biscuits and teas.

5 HARRODS

87–135 Brompton Rd,
SW1X 7XL
020 7730 1234
www.harrods.com
Open Mon–Sat 10am–9pm,
Sun 11.30am–6pm
Tube Knightsbridge
[MAP p. 170 A2]

One of the world's grandest
and most famous department
stores, Harrods is a genteel
(but crowded) reminder of
elegant shopping. Staff in
straw boaters and striped
aprons look the part in Harrods'
upmarket food hall, which is so
bountiful with produce it could
work as a market scene in a
movie styled by Baz Luhrmann.
Whole fish and shiny orange
crustaceans laze over blocks
of ice, tiered cakes burst at
the seams with cream and
strawberries and the smells of
rich dark cacao, fresh ground
coffee and biscuits permeate
the air as you stroll around.
The eye candy doesn't stop
there – with lavish interiors
throughout. Each department –
be it menswear, womenswear,
shoes, international and
Brit fashion – is creatively
curated to evoke a fashion
studio or catwalk show. The
womenswear, especially, is
exquisite, from the world's
best designers, with prices
to match – true fashionistas
will head here. Travellers
often buy Harrods-branded
shopping bags and teddy
bear souvenirs.

97

6 HARVEY NICHOL∫

109–125 Knightsbridge;
SW1X 7RJ
020 7235 5000
www.harveynichols.com
Open Mon–Sat 10am–8pm,
Sun 11.30am–6pm
Tube Knightsbridge
[MAP p. 170 B1]

Head-turning edgy shop
windows with mannequins
kitted out in featured designers
have always given Harvey
Nichols kudos in the fashion
world. Inclusion in the store
catalogue can make or break
a label. But it's a fickle game,
fashion. Harvey Nics, founded
in 1831, is revamping its first
floor to further showcase
international brands (Essentiel
Amsterdam is my favourite).
Unlike nearby Harrods
(see p. 97) Harvey Nics is a
dedicated fashion store, but
the two compete when it
comes to showing off the latest
look. There are stylists on hand,
and the sunny rooftop fifth
floor has a food hall where you
can buy gifty food products
like artisan salts, smart looking
drink bottles, couture cook
books, truffle and artisan
chocolate. If nothing else, just
go here to observe how real,
wealthy Londoners shop.

POCKET TIP
Harvey Nichols is on the
corner of Sloane Street, an
upmarket shopping street
that leads to Sloane Square
and more shopping on
Kings Road, Chelsea.

7 FOOD FILOƒOPHY

9 Kinnerton St, SW1X 8EA
Open Mon–Fri 7.30am–6pm
Tube Knightsbridge
[MAP p. 171 E4]

Take a stroll down one of Knightsbridge's attractive and serene back streets, where flower pots hang outside enviable terraced apartments, to Food Filosophy, a cafe dishing out Greek-inspired dishes. The space is clean, white and contemporary with a sunken, white marble food counter abundantly laid-out with platters of grilled salmon fillets, spinach and feta filo pastries, meatballs and grilled marinated chicken pieces. The idea is to choose one of these mains, then pair it with, say the taramasalata or hummus dip, and two or three hearty salads. Tomato and butter bean, cucumber and dahl, green bean and Greek salads were some of the options on my last visit. Seating is minimal especially given the lunchtime crowd here.

POCKET TIP

If there are no seats available at Food Filosophy, another (cheaper) option is to take-away to Hyde Park (see p. 94) for a picnic lunch.

8 THE ALFRED TENNYSON

10 Motcomb St, SW1X 8LA
020 7730 6074
www.thealfredtennyson.co.uk
Open Mon–Thurs 8am–11pm,
Fri 8am–11.30pm, Sat 9am–
11.30pm, 9am–10.30pm
Tube Knightsbridge
[MAP p. 170 C2]

Designer poodles and Botox bottoms can be spotted at this Knightsbridge darling, but don't be put off. This is one of those charismatic but contemporary English pubs that feels freshly painted and new despite being in a gloriously old building. The kitchen shares the same approach, serving up traditional English fare with modern farm-to-table aplomb. Interesting starters, such as gin and tonic cured salmon with crème fraîche and pickled shallots, can be followed with stalwart mains, like battered fish and chips with crushed peas and tartare. Sunday roasts – breed beef sirloin, Middle White pork and Hebridean lamb – make my mouth water just writing about them. The drinks list features whimsically named drinks such as Aspall 'Harry Sparrow' Cider and Beavertown 'Neck Oil' Session IPA. One really could stay all day.

POCKET TIP
Head southeast down Motcomb Street for an eye-full of boutiques, including Lowndes, Christian Louboutin and Pierre Hermé Paris.

9 EGERTON HOU/E HOTEL

17–19 Egerton Terrace, SW3 2BX
020 7589 2412
www.egertonhousehotel.com
Open Mon–Sun 12pm–6pm
(afternoon tea)
Tube South Kensington
[MAP p. 173 E1]

Marvellously British is one way of describing this exquisitely intimate bar hidden on a terraced street in boutique Egerton House Hotel. The place feels so jolly gosh welcoming it's like being in the drawing room of a posh and hospitable English friend. Treat yourself to afternoon tea served on three-tiered silver platters while you sit in a high back lounge chair amid antique clocks, plush furniture, a gallery of framed artworks and, if you're lucky, a posh poodle (dogs are as complimentary to the setting as the gilt-framed mirrors and bevelled plastering). The house-made bread finger sandwiches layered with cream cheese and salmon top even the chocolate macaron for taste. Esley, the bonhomie lifer barman, also draws a crowd with his gin and vodka martinis. They're not shaken or stirred – rather, the spirit is chilled at minus 22 degrees Celsius, then served in an icy glass with a shake of vermouth and spritz of lemon. It knocked my socks off, by Jove.

POCKET TIP
Many of London's grand hotels serve traditional afternoon tea in elegant surrounds. A visit to the British capital wouldn't be complete without one.

101

SOUTH KENSINGTON

South Kensington might have the affluence of its Knightsbridge neighbour, but it also has the riches bound up in the extraordinary collections of some of London's major cultural, artistic and historic attractions. The V&A (Victoria and Albert Museum, *see* p. 104) will give you enough art and design inspiration to last a lifetime; the Natural History Museum (*see* p. 107) is a drawcard for David Attenborough-types and dinosaur fans; and the Science Museum (*see* p. 107) is great fun and interactive even if you're not travelling with kids. Better still, all three museums are free. Nearby Kensington Palace (*see* p. 106), in verdant Kensington Gardens, combines royal history with one of London's most beautiful areas for a stroll.

South Ken's shops and boutiques – the Conran Shop (*see* p. 108) being the crowd favourite – are high-end but designer cool. Its restaurants can be pricey, but there are still venues where a Sunday roast or an age-dried steak is affordable. For the budget-conscious traveller, there are eateries clustered around South Kensington Tube station, Gloucester Road Tube station, down side streets and on the roads between Cromwell Road and Kensington High Street. South Ken is a central and elegant precinct to stay in or visit.

Tube: South Kensington, Gloucester Road, High Street Kensington

↤ *The Sunken Garden at Kensington Palace is a serene place to spend time*

SIGHTS
1. V&A (Victoria & Albert Museum)
2. Kensington Palace
3. Natural History Museum

SHOPPING
4. The Conran Shop

EATING
5. Comptoir Libanais
6. Macellaio RC

EATING & DRINKING
7. Stables Bar
8. The Britannia

1 V&A (VICTORIA & ALBERT MUSEUM)

Cromwell Rd, SW7 2RL
020 7942 2000
www.vam.ac.uk
Open Sat–Thurs 10am–
5.45pm, Fri 10am–11pm
Tube South Kensington
[MAP p. 173 D2]

Another of London's freebie
destinations is the V&A
(Victoria and Albert), a
world-beating museum of
art and design that boasts
an extraordinary permanent
collection of more than
2.3 million objects. Spanning
5000 years of creativity, you
can see everything from
Alexander McQueen dresses to
ancient Japanese and Korean
art. It's worthy of many visits,
but if you only come once,
choose, say, the fashion room,
showcasing the history of
dress up until the 21st century.
Some of my favourite rooms
include the cast courts and
the Raphael Cartoons. The
temporary exhibitions are
popular so book ahead. Don't
miss the V&A shop, where
exhibition-inspired books,
bags and colourful gifts have
a design-edge. If you need
sustenance while viewing
beautiful objects, head to the
equally appealing William
Morris-designed rooms for
tea and cake.

2 KENSINGTON PALACE ✓

Kensington Gardens, W8 4PX
020 3166 6000
www.hrp.org.uk/kensington-palace
Open 10am–6pm (Mar–Oct),
10am–4pm (Nov–Feb)
Tube High Street Kensington
[MAP p. 174 C2]

The official residence of royals William and Kate and co, and now Harry and Meghan, is, quite remarkably, also accessible to the public. A stroll through the sumptuous oak-lined **Broad Walk** has you passing the front gate like you might pop in for a cuppa, although their royal highnesses won't be answering the door. Entry into the public rooms, including the **State Apartments**, is a royalist's flight of fancy. Explore the glittering court of George II and Queen Caroline; and idle around the oldest part of the palace in the intimate rooms of Queen Mary II, who ruled with her husband King William III. Also, see how Queen Vic spent her childhood here before her 67-year reign as queen. The Palace hosts major exhibitions such as *Diana: Her Fashion Story*, which attracted much attention.

POCKET TIP

The serene and aromatic Sunken Garden, at the front of the palace, was a favourite of Diana's and has been transformed into The White Garden in her memory. It's free.

POCKET TIP

Just up Exhibition Road is the Science Museum, with incredible exhibitions and interactive displays on space, engineering, mathematics, technology and our planet.

3 NATURAL HISTORY MUSEUM

Cromwell Rd, SW7 5BD
020 7942 5000
www.nhm.ac.uk
Open Mon–Sun 10am–5.30pm
Tube South Kensington
[MAP p. 172 B2]

So wrapped in intrigue is the city's largest repository of historical artefacts (including the remains of 58 million animals), that the museum's grandiose central room has been the setting for movies including *Night at the Museum* and *Paddington* (picture a runaway Paddington sliding down the stair bannister). But this is more than just movies, it's real life – or should I say death. From the 25-metre-long blue whale skeleton floating above you in the entry to the taxidermy animals and the roaring life-sized T-rex, this is a natural world boffin's wonderland. David Attenborough has been digitally recreated as a lifelike 3D hologram and hosts guided tours of the collection highlights. This attracts a small fee, as do other long-term exhibitions such as the dreamy butterfly enclosure, but otherwise the museum is one of London's great free-entry destinations. If you're here in November or December, there's an ice-skating rink; during summer, the pond provides water-play for kids.

4 THE CONRAN SHOP

Michelin House, 81 Fulham Rd,
SW3 6RD
020 7589 7401
www.conranshop.co.uk
Open Mon–Tues & Fri 10am–
6pm, Wed–Thurs 10am–7pm,
Sat 10am–6.30pm, Sun
12pm–6pm
Tube South Kensington
[MAP p. 173 E3]

The Conran name equates to
London's up-there architecture,
design and style. This flagship
store opened in 1987 in the
Art Deco Michelin House
building, the Michelin Tyre
Company's original British
headquarters. It continues
to be that one step ahead for
furniture, interior design and
homewares and is surrounded
by well-to-do neighbours that
can afford to pay the design
premium. For us travellers, the
store is a pleasure to browse in.
Anyone seeking retail therapy
can rest assured there's an
edit of useful and aesthetically
pleasing backpackable
wares, including notebooks
and journals, Plugbug world
chargers, reusable bags in
colourful patterns, Moses
slides (sandals), sunnies and
drink bottles.

POCKET TIP

Visit the Medici Gallery
(26 Thurloe St) for beautiful
stationery, South Kensington
Books (22 Thurloe St) and
Skandium (35 Thurloe
Place) for Scandi-
homewares.

5 COMPTOIR LIBANAIʃ

1–5 Exhibition Rd, SW7 2HE
020 7225 5006
www.comptoirlibanais.com
Open Mon–Sat 8.30am–12am,
Sun 8.30am–10.30pm
Tube South Kensington
[MAP p. 172 C2]

Middle Eastern decor mashes
it up with pop culture in
this lively Lebanese eatery
with 1950s' vinyl chairs,
a kaleidoscope of mosaic
tiles, coloured glass lamps,
silver coffee trays and – my
favourite – the playful frames
of Lady Diana and Barack
Obama sporting fez hats. Like!
The open kitchen, with big
vegetable pickle jars tickling
the ceiling, proffers a menu
bursting with Middle Eastern
favourites: lamb koftas and
kebabs, grilled haloumi salads
and falafel wraps. Or try a
mezze plate – they're fittingly
colourful with bright pink
beetroot labne dip, lime green
pickled jalapenos, pomegranate
topped hummus, pastries and
tabouli. The lemonade here
is homemade and laden with
syrupy flavours including rose,
orange blossom, mint and
ginger. This is a busy place,
but solo travellers have a good
chance to nab a stool with a
view outside.

POCKET TIP
Comptoir Libanais
eateries have popped
up across London.
There's one nearby at
77a Gloucester Rd,
South Kensington.

6 MACELLAIO RC

84 Old Brompton Rd, SW7 3LQ
020 7589 5834
www.macellaiorc.com
Open Mon–Thurs 12pm–3pm
6–11pm, Fri–Sat 12pm–11pm,
Sun 12pm–10.30pm
Tube South Kensington
[MAP p. 172 B4]

If you only have one steak in London, have it here. These guys specialise in dry-ageing their meat, the evidence of which hangs, a little purple and gruesome, from meat hooks in the front window. Inside, the decor is a cross between butcher shop and Italian bistro, the beef-cut crowded deli counter and white butcher tiles softened by wooden tables set with red serviettes. Italian Fassone (cattle) beef is the specialty, and it's hung to perfection for six weeks, allowing the taste and texture to develop. It's melt-in-the-mouth stuff whether you have it as a carpaccio starter or as a rump steak drizzled with Ligurian olive oil. Beef is the main game, but grilled rabbit, roast baby chicken and pasta al pomodoro are given equal attention. My brother-in-law, who hails from the Italian Dolomite region, was spot-on with this recommendation.

7 STABLES BAR

The Milestone Hotel
1 Kensington Court, W8 5DL
020 7917 1000
www.milestonehotel.com
Open Mon–Sun 10am–11pm
Tube High Street Kensington
[MAP p. 174 C3]

On a cold London night, when the chilled wind is whipping around the collars of your coat, duck off Kensington High Street into the warmth of The Stables bar, a hidey hole in a corner of the 17th-century-built Milestone Hotel. As the name suggests, this was the hotel's old stables, and the equine theme continues with framed horse paintings and polished horse-shoes, tastefully adorning a tiny room with wood-panelled walls, luscious green-striped carpet and green leather couches. Ever-professional and friendly, the bar staff, wearing white jackets and black ties, take their beverages seriously. The Old Fashion, made from a New Orleans' recipe with 60-year-old whisky barrel-aged in Canadian maple syrup and vodka, is the house specialty. The bar snacks, with olives, toasted sandwiches, rarebit and dips with pickled vegetables, are a tasty English-twist accompaniment to any cocktail they can conjure.

POCKET TIP

Nearby, Japan House (101–111 Kensington High St) is an ode to all-things Nippon: design, innovation, technology and gastronomy.

8 THE BRITANNIA

1 Allen Street, W8 6UX
020 7937 6905
www.britanniakensington.co.uk
Open Mon–Sat 11am–12am,
Sun 11am–11pm
Tube High Street Kensington
[MAP p. 174 B4]

Goose-fat potatoes, double-egg Yorkshire puddings and honey-roasted heritage cabbage – if you're looking for a traditional British roast dinner, you've found the place, and that's before we've talked about the meat. Choose between 21-day-aged sirloin beef, half a chicken stuffed with chorizo, rolled pork belly with apple sauce, or, and this is almost wrong, a trio of all three. This pub, in an old brewery building, from circa 1834, has all the low-slung ceiling nostalgia of an old drinking den with the comforts and decor of a cosy lounge – leather couches and fabric-covered chairs, flowers in vases, throw cushions and soft lighting make this a winsome place to settle in. There are other classic dishes on the menu, but with a dozen or so draught beers and staff with a penchant for rum-based cocktails, you're welcome to a drinking session too.

POCKET TIP
Visit Kensington High Street for outdoor/travel stores, chain fashion brands and a Wholefoods (no. 63–97) for picnic supplies to take to nearby Kensington Gardens.

NOTTING HILL

This West London suburb, so well marketed by the famed rom-com of the same name, is trendy, high-end, once bohemian and now probably full of bankers (with apologies to my once-resident Aussie brother-in-law), but it manages to retain its heart and soul. For this we can thank Portobello Road Market (*see* p. 118), the uber-popular antiques-and-everything-else market that extends over a dozen blocks down the centre of Notting Hill every day of the week. The same shopkeepers and market traders have been plying their trade here for decades, and the tourists it attracts have been a leverage for iconic shops, like The Spice Shop (*see* p. 123) and Books for Cooks (*see* p. 122), to maintain a trade.

Take a walk down Westbourne Grove – its clothing boutiques and white-tabled cafes are a picture of well-heeled serenity. It's an idyllic precinct to meander around, with its coloured terrace houses and private, walled gardens to peep into. And if you chance upon Notting Hill Carnival in August, prepare to party. Hard.

Tube: Notting Hill Gate, Ladbroke Grove

→ *With its floral facade, the Churchill Arms is a nostalgic nod to the former British prime minister*

SIGHTS
1. Portobello Road Market

SHOPPING
2. Couverture & the Garbstore
3. Books for Cooks
4. The Spice Shop

SHOPPING & EATING
5. Daylesford Organic

EATING
6. Andina Panaderia & Picanteria
7. Tonkotsu

DRINKING
8. Ginstitute
9. The Churchill Arms

1 PORTOBELLO ROAD MARKET

Portobello Rd
www.portobelloroad.co.uk
Open Mon–Wed 9am–6pm,
Thurs 9am–1pm, Fri–Sat
9am–7pm
Tube Notting Hill Gate,
Ladbroke Grove
[MAP p. 176 B3]

Lined with colourful terrace houses, extending almost from Notting Hill Gate to Ladbroke Grove, and awash each Saturday with a sea of heads, this famed market is a must-do. It's one of the world's largest antiques markets with more than 1000 dealers, but a walk from top to bottom reveals fruit and veg stalls, vintage fashion, flea-market wares, new boutiques and more. That said, the antiques are the most intriguing. Find yourself old brass and leather travel trunks at **Henry Gregory**; opal pendant necklaces and western boots at **Jessie Western**; old clocks, porcelain teapots and glass door handles at **The Blue Door**; colourful carpet bags from **Appletree Boutique**; and indomitably British tailor-made tweed jackets at **Stumped and Fielding**. And don't miss **Alice's**. This bright red corner shop filled with dusty ephemera is the stuff of storybooks and movies.

POCKET TIP

Friday is the second biggest market day – you'll get atmosphere but fewer people. If you go Saturday, arrive before 11.30am to avoid crowds.

119

2 COUVERTURE & THE GARB/TORE

188 Kensington Park Rd,
W11 2ES
020 7229 2178
www.couvertureandthegarb
store.com
Open Mon–Sat 10am–6pm,
Sun 12pm–5pm
Tube Ladbroke Grove
[MAP p. 176 A2]

In the *Sound of Music*, when
Julie Andrews does that
smiling, hands in the air,
spinning around thing – that's
what I feel like when I visit this
clothing boutique. Every dress,
every jumper, every cushion,
every handbag in stock is
selected for the artistic,
aesthetic and tactile pleasure it
radiates. You can walk around
the two levels here in the kind
of rapture you'd normally save
for an art exhibition. Of course,
this means it's no bargain
centre, more a place to buy
that birthday gift-to-self or
outfit for that special person's
upcoming nuptials. Fork out
for a floral jacquard skirt, a
sheepskin coat, a smock raglan
sleeve dress or a cashmere
snood. Downstairs is The
Garbstore, the men's edit with
equally tasteful and expertly
presented modern men's garb
including plaid shirts, cotton
flannels, trainers and special
edition sandals.

COUVERTURE &
THE GARBSTORE

The new
collection

3 BOOKƧ FOR COOKƧ

4 Blenheim Cres, W11 1NN
020 7221 1992
www.booksforcooks.com
Open Tues–Sat 10am–6pm
Tube Ladbroke Grove
[MAP p. 176 A2]

I'm a bit of a cookbook junkie and this famed shop is my go-to for a hit. It's diminutive and un-showy, but it has managed to survive the fickle book scene for 35 years, such is its following. With more than 8000 titles in stock its jam-packed, colourful book spines reach the ceiling and the latest releases – all hard-backed and beautifully designed – crowd a central table. Dig out popular English cooking classics like Delia's *Complete Cookery Course* or scout around for modern favourites, such as Diana Henry's *How to Eat a Peach* and Rukmini Iyer's Roasting Tin series. Aside from cookbooks this is the place to find foodie fiction, history and nutrition, and the owners are happy to scour the globe for titles yet to hit their shelves. At the back of the shop is a kitchen where book recipes are tested and a **cafe** where the successes (presumably) are sold. They also nail a decent latte.

POCKET TIP

Lutyens & Rubinstein (21 Kensington Park Road) is an indie Notting Hill bookstore owned by literary agents.

4 THE SPICE SHOP

1 Blenheim Cres, W11 2EE
020 7221 4448
www.thespiceshop.co.uk
Open Mon–Sat 9.30am–6pm,
Sun 11am–3pm
Tube Ladbroke Grove
[MAP p. 176 B2]

Amchoor, aniseeds, annatto seeds, asafoetida, basil, bay leaf, black onion seeds, caraway seeds, cardamom pods … I could fill this review with a list of the herbs and spices stocked in this aromatic bolthole 10 times over. Opened in 1995 by Birgit Erath, after five years trading at Portobello Road Market (see p. 118), this tiny stall-sized space has become another of London's iconic shops. Its sunflower-yellow shopfront, adorned with five or six humble vegie-filled baskets and ropes of hanging garlic, is repeated indoors where more than 2500 herbs, spices and blends are lined up on the shelves, many of them in gorgeous retro red and yellow tins. Over the years, Birgit's rep as a spice trader and blender has grown and her shop is the source of inspiration for world-famous chefs. She says favourites tend to be seasonal 'but Moroccan raz el hanout and Penang Coconut Curry are always in demand'.

POCKET TIP
You might catch Birgit running one of the cooking classes at Books for Cooks (see p. 122) over the road.

123

5 DAYLE**S**FORD ORGANIC

208–212 Westbourne Grove,
W11 2RH, UK
020 7313 8050
www.daylesford.com
Open Mon 8am–7pm, Tues–Sat
8am–9.30pm, Sun 10am–4pm
Tube Notting Hill Gate
[MAP p. 177 D3]

I had my first avocado smoothie from this wholesome organic eatery and produce store when it opened 10 years ago; the well-to-do owner was stocking it with mindful and sustainable products before soy lattes were a thing. Breakfast is especially good with buzz words like Bircher, market garden, hand-cut, outdoor-reared and cold-pressed garnishing the menu. The eggs Benedict has thick cut ham from pigs reared in the Daylesford farm in Gloucestershire and the omelette is layered with asparagus and peas snipped from the farm in the Cotswolds (both worthwhile visits if you're in the region). Tables outside are perfect for people-watching, but inside is a full immersion among mounds of sourdough loaves, pyramids of jams, jars of pickles and packets of cookies. There's a homewares basement for linen teatowels, aprons, kitchenware, candles and decorative wares.

POCKET TIP

Nearby, try vegetarian guru Ottolenghi (63 Ledbury Rd), lifestyle store Aime (32 Ledbury Rd) and Ladbroke Arms gastro-pub (54 Ladbroke Grove).

6 ANDINA PANADERIA & PICANTERIA

155–157 Westbourne Grove,
W11 2RS
020 3327 9465
www.cevichefamily.com
Open Mon–Fri 12pm–11.30pm,
Sat–Sun 10am–11.30pm
Tube Notting Hill Gate
[MAP p. 177 F3]

Andina founder Martin Morales is responsible for bringing Peruvian food to London. This venture celebrates the soulful cooking of Andean picanterias (street food eateries). Nutritious and native dishes include tasty chicharron (fried pork belly sandwich) and small plates including a tuna tartare prettily adorned with avocado cream, fish roe and dehydrated beetroot. The decor is similarly colourful with wool cushions, green and purple velour bench seats and wall-hangings featuring traditional Andean women. The bakery, Andina Panaderia, is devoted to slow-fermented, handcrafted Peruvian baking. The result is braided pastry anise-flavoured rosquita, crispy sweet-topped pastel de lucuma and savoury tres puntas (three-point) rolls. The duo of shops has got you covered for coffee, brunch, lunch or dinner.

7 TONKOT/U

7 Blenheim Cres, W11 2EE
020 7221 8300
www.tonkotsu.co.uk
Open Sun–Thurs 11.30am–
10.30pm, Fri–Sat 11.30am–11pm
Tube Ladbroke Grove
[MAP p. 176 A2]

A few years ago, London was hit with a ramen craze and shops selling ginormous bowls of Japanese pork-bone broth and noodles proliferated across the city. Tonkotsu is one of the success stories with a handful of incarnations for informal eating. The Notting Hill version is a slip of an eatery with Japanese authenticity. Guests are hustled to stools at the bar, overlooking a narrow kitchen where the chefs rattle around with woks and containers of pre-prepped ingredients. The menu is simple and reasonably priced with four ramen varieties, including three kinds of house-made noodles – the eponymous tonkotsu being one of them – plus pork belly, seafood, chicken and vegan curried pumpkin options. Start with gyozas, edamame and pickles, and end with my favourite Japanese dessert – mochi balls, delicious Japanese confectionery with an ice-cream centre.

8 GIN/TITUTE

186 Portobello Rd, W11 1LA
020 3034 2233
www.the-distillery.london
Open Mon–Sat 11am–12pm,
Sun 11am–11pm
Tube Ladbroke Grove
[MAP p. 176 B2]

Notoriously bustling Portobello Road needs places like the Ginstitute, where you can slip away and sip away all the while watching the crowd. This fully functioning distillery provides four floors of high-spirited activity in a gorgeous 19th-century corner building. There are three cheerful boutique guestrooms (with copper cocktail shakers in the mini bars), an upbeat Basque restaurant and a basement distillery room, which plays hosts to gin master classes and the popular street-level **Resting Room**. This cocktail bar is *the* place for a refined aged Scotch whiskey, an unheard-of Spanish Sherry or an Old Tom Gin which is created on-site and served fresh off the 400 litre copper pot still called King Henry. My pick is the Gin Sour. It's made from lemon, sugar, egg whites and the distillery's Portobello Road Gin, a bottle of which makes for a great local souvenir.

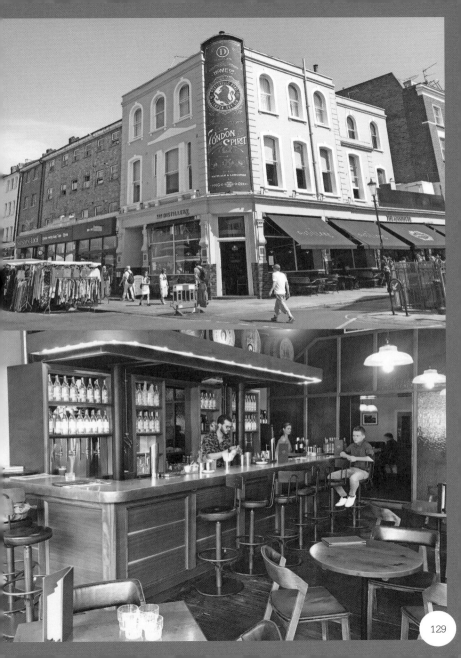

9 THE CHURCHILL ARMS

119 Kensington Church St,
W8 7LN
020 7727 4242
www.churchillarmskensington.
co.uk
Open Mon–Wed 11am–11pm,
Thurs–Sat 11am–12am,
Sun 12pm–10.30pm
Tube Notting Hill Gate
[MAP p. 174 B2]

Care for a real ale? Churchill is your man. This is an old school English boozer, the kind where you can sit at a tiny table and sink six pints and nobody will look at you sideways. It's also rather eccentric. The entire corner facade blooms with pink pansies and red geraniums, so that most folk know it as the 'pub covered in flowers'. Inside, it's intriguing with memorabilia to duck and dive around. Old copper kitchen pans and gas lanterns hang from the ceiling alongside Union Jack bunting. The walls are crammed with framed war-themed newspaper articles, sepia-tinged photos of Churchill and models of old war planes. The pub, built in 1750, is one of London's oldest, and the story goes that Churchill's grandparents were visitors here in the 1800s, which accounts for the name that came about post-World War II. This is a little British nugget worth stepping into.

POCKET TIP

Kensington Church Street runs from Notting Hill Gate to Kensington High Street and is full of antique and interior stores to browse gallery-style window displays.

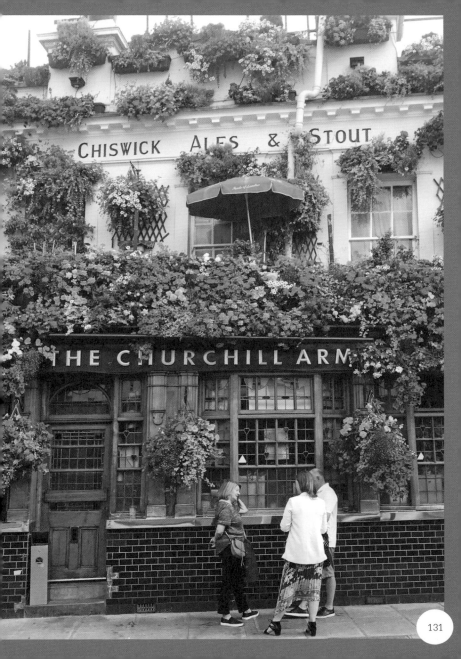

FIELD TRIP

BATH

Ninety minutes by train from London, the city of Bath – a UNESCO Cultural World Heritage Site, is a dreamy destination for a romantic escape from London. And that's not to say you need a lover to come here – it's the city itself that imbues any stay with a crimson blush. This is the home of literature great Jane Austen, one of the first romantic novelists. Bath, the city she wrote about in the early 1800s, is still here in the sandy colour Georgian architecture of grandiose terraced streets, such as Royal Crescent and the Circus, a circle of three-storey terraces built around an internal garden. Bath was a fashionable spa town in Austen's day, and this too remains the same. Its ancient Roman Baths (see p. 136), which date back to AD70, boast about being the best-preserved Roman remains in the world. Uniquely in the UK, they produce a hot thermal water which rises to the surface at a constant temperature of 46 degrees Celsius. These mineral-rich waters have given rise to therapeutic day spas, like Thermae (see p. 134), and have made the city a global magnet for those keen on a soak. Bath has many shops and eateries, verdant surrounding countryside and makes for a memorable daytrip from London or a longer stay.

Trains leave from London Paddington to Bath on average 35 times a day.

→ *Pulteney Bridge on the River Avon*

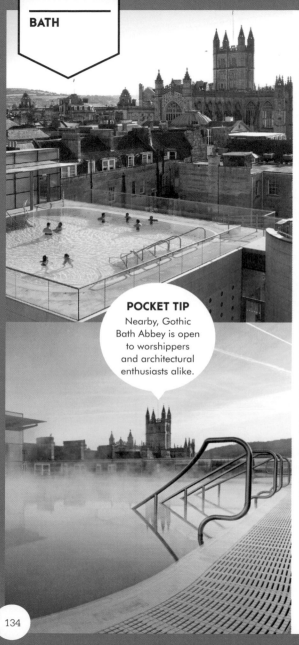

POCKET TIP

Nearby, Gothic Bath Abbey is open to worshippers and architectural enthusiasts alike.

THERMAE BATH SPA

Hetling Pump Room,
Hot Bath St, BA1 1SJ
012 2533 1234
www.thermaebathspa.com
Open daily 9am–7.30pm
(main spa)

On a chilly morning, with the steam rising thick, there's no better place to be than immersed in Thermae's open-air rooftop pool, soaking up the mineral-rich hot thermal waters in much the same way the Romans did. Save perhaps for the setting. This contemporary square-shaped pool sits atop a modern stone-and glass-clad building in the very heart of the city's heritage precinct. The sleek-lined perspex fencing enables guests to ogle the Gothic pinnacles of Bath Abbey, and the chimney pots of the city's Georgian architecture. A two-hour spa session with access to a wellness suite and indoor pool is the baseline offering, but guests could go all out choosing one of 40 beauty treatments and packages that could keep you settled in for a week. Best to book ahead for treatments.

POCKET TIP

En route from London to Bath, explore Wiltshire and the famed stone circles: Stonehenge or Avebury, or marvel at one of the hillside white horses.

JANE AUSTEN CENTRE

40 Gay St, Queen Square, BA1 2NT
012 2544 3000
www.janeausten.co.uk
Open daily 9.45am–5.30/6pm (summer); Mon–Fri & Sun 10am–4pm, Sat 10.45am–5.30pm (winter)

'Oh! Who can ever be tired of Bath?' exclaims Catherine, the protagonist in Austen's *Northanger Abbey* novel, written in 1803. Touché! To read up on Bath before arrival, there are no better books than *Northanger Abbey* and *Persuasion*, in which Bath is the principal city. Failing that, drop by the Jane Austen Centre in a classic Georgian townhouse on a street that Austen once lived on. The permanent exhibition is a bit cheesy, with staff dressed in Regency costume, but it's informative in a friendly way. Explore the influence the city had on her works through talks, activities and film screenings, and take a gander at a waxwork of the novelist herself. Austen's intriguing unpublished manuscripts are also on display. Upstairs there's a **tea room** decked out in Regency style, with a selection of teas, scones and sandwiches. In the **gift shop**, it's hard to go past the 'I dream of Mr Darcy' (i.e. Colin Firth) pillowcase.

POCKET TIP

Near Bath, also in the county of Somerset, is the beautiful 19th-century garden of Stourhead.

ROMAN BATHS

The Roman Baths, Abbey Church Yard, BA1 1LZ
012 2547 7785
www.romanbaths.co.uk
Open Mon–Sun 9am–6pm (Jan–Oct), Mon–Sun 9am–10pm (Jun–Aug), 9.30am–6pm (Nov–Dec)

About 1,170 000 litres of mineral-rich thermal water, at a burning 46° Celsius, streams into the Roman Baths each day, much as it did when the baths were constructed around AD70. You can't swim here (this is one of only two Roman baths in the world with hot water flowing into it, so it's rather precious), but the extensive ruins are almost mystically evocative of a time when people did. At the centre of the complex is the main Roman bath – a 1.6-metre deep pool with well-worn steps leading down on all sides. Around it, Roman columns on plinths, decorative stone balustrading, arches and statues, all give a sense of the historical significance of the site. In the old changing rooms and saunas, this is heightened by lifelike wall projections that reflect the bathing scene in ancient times. There's also a fountain where you can taste the water – it has 43 minerals in it.

THE
ROMAN BATHS

THE
ROMAN BATHS

POCKET TIP
Beyond Bath are numerous picturesque villages, such as Castle Combe and the market town of Bradford on Avon.

BRIGHTON

Hands-down one of the best places to live in the UK outside London and a great escape out of the capital, seaside Brighton shines with a combination of heritage charm, beachside kitsch and hipster cool. Or should that be heritage kitsch, beachside cool and hipster charm? Whichever way you look at it, this is a party town with a fashionable and historic past that makes it comfortable humming to the sound of its own little eccentricities. You can go from a thriller roller-coaster ride on Brighton Palace Pier (see p. 140) to the Mughal-style minareted Royal Pavilion (see p. 142) in minutes and nothing seems out of place. For a real Brighton buzz, experience a day on the pebble beach in all its nostalgic excess. By night, take to the streets to check out on-trend fine-diners, antiquated pubs, indie eateries and late-night bars. Brighton is also known as the UK's LGBTIQ capital with gay-friendly bars that have been around for decades.

A train trip from London takes one hour, making it one of the city's easiest getaways. You could jump on the train from Victoria, London Bridge or St Pancras and be on the beach in time for a fake tan to set in. In summer, everyone is thinking the same thing so expect a crowd but a party too. Good times.

→ *Seaside Brighton has lively and colourful streets*

139

POCKET TIP

Big Fish Trading Company at the entry to the pier do a crunchy battered fish with a worthy salt and vinegar chip accompaniment.

BRIGHTON PALACE PIER

Madeira Drive, BN2 1TW
012 7360 9361
www.brightonpier.co.uk
Open Mon–Fri 10am–8pm, Sat 10am–8pm, Sun 10am–7pm

For some old-school fairground fun, come one, come all to Brighton's tackiest attraction, a 525-metre-long historic structure that juts out into the water from Brighton Beach. Tacky it might be, but the pier, with its plank floors, central dome and decorative weatherboard buildings, attracts more than 4.5 million visitors a year. They come in all weather for side-show attractions and dozens of rides – from a thrill-seeker's turbo roller-coaster to a quaint gold-spangled carousel. If fun parks aren't your thing, the pier still merits a visit for its old-school charm and to see how people were entertained in bygone days. If offers fetching views back towards Brighton Beach, so grab yourself a striped deck chair and enjoy a view over surprisingly blue water to a pebbly beach (that's right – no sand) busy with towel-wielding sun-soakers. Behind it, a string of charming white wedding-cake style apartment blocks extends along the foreshore. It's pretty as a picture.

ROYAL PAVILION

4/5 Pavilion Buildings, BN1 1EE
030 0029 0900
www.brightonmuseums.org.uk
Open Mon–Sun 10am–5.15pm
(Oct–Mar), Mon–Sun 9.30am–
5.45pm (Apr–Sep)

Welcome to India, circa 1823.
Err, rather England, circa 1823.
This exceptionally ornate and
opulent building, decorated
with domes and minarets in
the style of palaces popular in
India during the 19th century,
was constructed as a seaside
residence for the Prince of
Wales, who later became King
George IV. Visitors can strut
through the lavish reception
rooms, royal bedrooms and
galleries, but don't miss the
latest addition: the recently
restored (it took three years)
saloon of George IV, an
incandescent display of vivid
red fabrics heavily brocaded
in gold silk, silver walls,
and furnishings featuring
dragons and palm trees. In the
pavilion garden buildings, the
**Brighton Museum and
Gallery** has diverse collections
both historic and current,
including 20th-century
design, fashion and fine art.
It's also renowned for its
LGBTIQ exhibitions.

POCKET TIP
Explore Brighton's
laneways full of chain
and indie stores, cafes,
bars and street art.

TERRE A TERRE

The Vegetarian Restaurant
71 East St, BN1 1HQ
012 73729 051
www.terreaterre.co.uk
Open Mon–Thurs 12pm–10pm,
Fri 12pm–10.30pm, Sat 11am–
10.30pm, Sun 11am–10pm

This vegetarian restaurant isn't faddish or trendy; its owners have been dishing out goodness – sustainable food minus the protein – since 1993. A solid customer-base of vegetarians and carnivores are still around for a reason. The owners, both chefs, win awards for their creative and thoughtful food, as well as plaudits for their ethical stance on food waste. We're not talking bowls of lentils on the menu either. In the spacious diner, with wood chairs and red canvas hangings, guests are served the likes of Korean fried cauliflower with pickled mirin ginger jelly followed by Szechuan-marinated haloumi and ginger bok choy bao served in a steamer. Desserts are prettily plated with crushed meringue and petal garnishes that leave, like this restaurant, a heavenly taste in your mouth.

HENLEY-ON-THAMES

Henley is Thames River county, with the main event being the 175-year-old festive and famous Henley Rowing Regatta in July each year. But the historic riverside town, with its Georgian shopfronts, market square and boutique shopping, is a great city escape any time. *Wind in the Willows*, the classic children's book by Kenneth Grahame, was inspired by the river country around Henley, and the bucolic scenes it portrays are still in evidence today – hedge rows, wooded forests, rolling meadows and bends in the river that reveal scenes of brambled country serenity. Holiday-makers come here to hire boats and barges for exploratory trips along the canals and river, but it's fantastically easy to 'mess about in boats' like Grahame's characters do on short trips with none of the regulations that hamper many water-based activities. And there's plenty for land-lubber activity, too. The Thames Path is perfect for an amble with river-related activities, like the River and Rowing Museum (*see* p. 148), along the way. The 13th-century Thursday Market still runs in Henley's main street. On the fourth Thursday and second Saturday, there's a farmer's market.

It's only an hour by train from London Paddington to Henley-on-Thames and trains run 40 times per day. The station plonks you within minutes of the action along the waterfront in the town centre.

→ *Tudor-style architecture, like that of The Angel, is part of Henley's charm*

HOBBS OF HENLEY

The Boat House, Station Rd,
RG9 1AZ
014 9157 2035
www.hobbsofhenley.com
Open Mon–Fri 8.30am–5pm
(Oct–Mar), Mon–Sun 8.30am–
6pm (Apr–Sep)

Cruising on the river is key to
a Henley visit. This family-
owned business, which has
been boating on the Thames
for near-on 150 years, offers a
dozen or so cruises, from gin
tours and afternoon teas on the
Mississippi paddle steamer-
style *New Orleans* vessel
to a wildlife cruise on the
Hibernia, a faster passenger
cruiser encased in glass. For
something more adventurous,
hire your own boat for a full day
or a couple of hours. There's a
choice of launches, the easiest
of which (aside from the
rowboats) is the Pearly class
outboard motor boats with
simple forward and backward
pedals. (Believe me, anyone
could do it). When you're all
aboard, putt under the Henley
Bridge toward Hambledon
Lock. This picturesque Thames
stretch has rolling meadows
either side and you can pull
in at idyllic **Temple Island**.
This folly, designed as a
fishing lodge, marks the start
of the famous Henley Royal
Regatta Course.

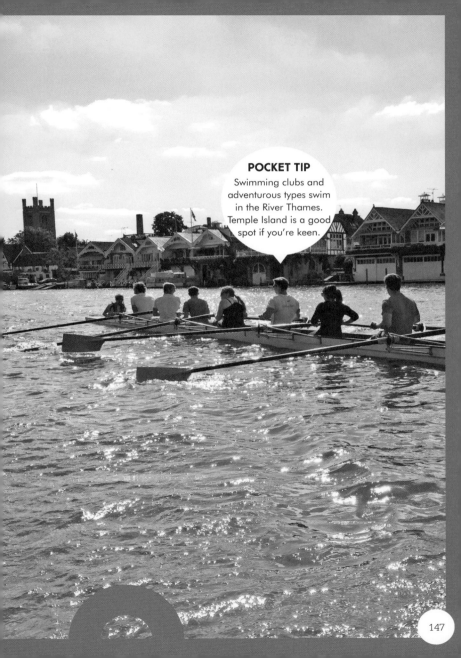

POCKET TIP

Swimming clubs and adventurous types swim in the River Thames. Temple Island is a good spot if you're keen.

RIVER & ROWING MUSEUM

Mill Meadows, RG9 1BF
014 9141 5600
www.rrm.co.uk
Open Mon–Sun 10am–5pm

If you walk south-east along the riverbank from Henley Bridge, you'll find Mills and Marsh Meadows, a green and pleasant parkland with a kids' adventure park, ducks to feed and sitting areas. At the end of the meadow the museum, an oak, glass and steel design resembling an upturned boat, has a 20,000-plus collection of photographs, historic books, ephemera, archive material and interactive exhibits on the history of the Thames Valley, the sport of rowing and the *Wild in the Willows* book. It also has a British art collection, including the works of those for whom the river has been a muse. It has a contemporary rather than fusty vibe, and there's something for everyone, including a *Wind in the Willows* 3D installation, a **gift shop** and **cafe**. In summer, Mills and Marsh Meadows amps up with jumping castles, ice-cream vans and deck chairs for hire.

POCKET TIP

For something more special, Hotel Du Vin has a cobbled courtyard and Champagne bar.

ANGEL ON THE BRIDGE

Thameside, RG9 1BH
014 9141 0678
www.theangelhenley.com
Open Mon–Sat 11am–12am,
Sun 11am–10.30pm

This old Tudor-style pub is not on the bridge, but it's as close to the beautiful five-arched 18th-century stone structure in the middle of Henley as it gets. It is the only pub overlooking the Thames in Henley so it draws a decent crowd. Sit riverside on a deck with 20 or so tables shaded by sun umbrellas (if it's sunny!) to watch swans and rowers glide past and boats tie up to the mooring. In winter, head indoors to the open fire in a cosy space with low ceilings and leather chairs serving real ales. The menu lists pub classics – Brakspear beer-battered haddock and chips, and Cumberland sausages with creamy mash and onion gravy; or step it up a culinary notch with fried fillet of seabass and lemon caper sauce or duck confit with sautéed thyme potatoes and spiced red cabbage. Choose small size portions of main meals if you're here for lunch.

GREENWICH

Greenwich is a Thames-side village that feels distant enough to be out of London but actually it's a south-east London borough, a UNESCO World Heritage Site that boasts some seriously grandiose buildings and maritime history. You've heard of Greenwich Mean Time (or GMT) in reference to the observance of time around the planet, well we have Greenwich's Royal Observatory (*see* p. 153) to thank for it. You can take a selfie on the meridian line or be mesmerised by a planetarium show, but there's so much to do here. From Greenwich Pier, the majestic *Cutty Sark* (*see* p. 152) tea clipper with its three towering masts, looms large and, beyond it, the town's maritime theme continues in the National Maritime Museum. The town centre itself has stone laneways, old pubs and undercover Greenwich Market (*see* p. 154), which evokes days when seafarers strolled the streets. The Queen's House, a formal royal residence built in the 17th century, houses an art collection that does both portraiture and contemporary painting to aplomb.

Greenwich is accessible from London from as far upriver as Putney (and 17 other stops along the way) on the Thames Clipper ferry service (www.thamesclippers.com). It is a worthy full day's outing. You can arrive by Tube too (though it's obviously not the scenic route) on the Jubilee line and Docklands Light Railway.

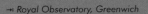

→ *Royal Observatory, Greenwich*

POCKET TIP

Grab a 50p map from the Tourist Information Centre and go on a self-guided 'architecture', 'viewpoints', 'royal' or 'highlights' tour.

CUTTY SARK

King William Walk, SE10 9HT
www.rmg.co.uk
Open Mon–Sun 10am–5pm

Looming large on the water's edge atop a glass encased visitor centre, the dry-docked *Cutty Sark*, built in 1869, was one of the last and fastest British tea clipper ships to be built before steam propulsion ships took over. In its heyday it sailed from London to China and back eight times in the tea trade, before becoming one of the fastest ships to carry wool back from Australia (the record was 73 days from Sydney to London). Its three towering masts, square rigs and narrow wooden hull with an iron frame cast a marvellous shadow over the Greenwich forecourt. You can step into the elaborate visitor centre where the *Cutty Sark*'s historic endeavours, marking the end of an era in sailing vessels, are narrated through artefacts, film, photos and interactive displays. Seafaring folk can also climb aboard to take the ship's helm, see how the crew lived and where the captain slept.

ROYAL OB/ERVATORY

Blackheath Avenue, SE10 8XJ
www.rmg.co.uk
Open Mon–Sun 10am–5pm

In 1884, with the help of
7th Astronomer Royal, Sir
George Biddell Airy, the
cross hairs in the Transit
Circle telescope at the Royal
Observatory precisely defined
Longitude 0 degrees – the
Prime Meridian that divides
the Earth's Eastern and
Western hemispheres (much
like the equator divides
the Northern and Southern
hemispheres). It's from this
meridian that Greenwich Mean
Time (GMT) – the observance
of time around the planet – is
established. You can celebrate
the achievement by dancing
from east to west across a
brass 'meridian line' (great
selfie op), and keep an eye out
for the green laser marking
it in the evening sky from
Greenwich Park hill towards
London's skyline. There's a
Time and Longitude gallery
exploring GMT's historic
journey, including a display of
historic timepieces. Better still,
head to the **Peter Harrison
Planetarium** and be
transported to another galaxy
via Mars.

POCKET TIP

On Greenwich main street, sweet-tooths take note: Peyton and Byrne for coffee and cupcakes; Hardy's Sweetshop for old-fashioned lollies.

GREENWICH MARKET

5B Greenwich Market,
SE10 9HZ
020 8269 5096
www.greenwichmarket.london
Open Mon–Sun 10am–5.30pm

Silver hip flasks, tea tins, Royal anniversary cups, army medals, colourful beads and bulky busts – this undercover market in the historic part of Greenwich village, a five-minute walk from the pier, is like a small version of the Portobello Road market (see p. 118). Its curios, antiques and ephemera are laid out on tables, so those of us intrigued by olde-worlde Britain can have a gander. The market's pint size is entirely welcoming, there are no crazy crowds that hamper the bigger markets and visitors can get around the stalls and the crafty shops that dot the outer edge without any fuss. The trading in British antiques might not have changed for decades, but the food offering has. At the other end of the market, **food trucks** selling a global selection of street food – Vietnamese banh mi rolls, American smoked barbeque pork brisket sandwiches and German snags – make lunch a must.

JOY

9 Nelson Rd, SE10 9JB
020 8293 7979
www.joythestore.com
Open Mon–Sun 10am–7pm

Britain's original fashion and lifestyle brand has been around for more than a decade, but it manages to keep its fresh and unique approach with colourful vintage-inspired women's and men's ware (polka dotted dresses, bold print shirts), eclectic gifts (stormtrooper decanter, Happy Socks) and quirky books (with life hack themes like 'Live, Love, Laugh' and 'How to be a Sloth'). It's a high street store with more than a dozen permutations in the UK, but each shop makes use of its original interiors for character and the best of them don't feel at all mainstream. The Greenwich shop retains the old fireplace surround, timber architraves and skylights of the Victorian building, and you could be forgiven for thinking it's owned by a Greenwich local.

POCKET TIP
The laneways around Joy are cobbled with little eateries and shops worth window-shopping.

155

TRAVEL TIPS

GETTING TO LONDON

You can enter the UK by plane, road (ferry) and train.

Plane

London Heathrow is the largest airport in Europe and is well connected to central London via the Underground (Tube) station network and the **Heathrow Express** (www.heathrowexpress.com) to London Paddington station (every 15–20 minutes). London Heathrow has five terminals so check your terminal before departure and arrival. Other international airports near London are **Gatwick**, **Stansted**, **London City** and **Luton**. All have public transport options to Central London: **Stansted Express** (www. standstedexpress.com) to London Liverpool Street station (every 15 minutes); **Gatwick Express** (www. gatwickexpress.com) to London Victoria station (four times per hour); **Docklands Light Rail** (www.tfl.gov.uk), part of the Tube network, leaves London City (every eight to 15 minutes); and trains leave **Luton Airport Parkway** (a 10-minute shuttle ride from Airport, (www.london-luton.co.uk) to Blackfriars, City Thameslink, Farringdon and St Pancras International stations every 10 minutes.

Road/Ferry

Car and passenger ferry services (aferry. com) link Britain with Europe. Portsmouth, Poole and Plymouth are the closest ports to London.

Train

The **Eurostar** train (Eurostar.com) links London's St Pancras station with the European continent (Paris, Lille and Calais in France, and Brussels in Belgium) via the Channel Tunnel. The Paris-to-London trip goes from Gare du Nord to St Pancras station and takes about two hours and twenty minutes. Pricewise, it's comparable to flying and it's far more convenient. Eurotunnel trains also take passengers in their cars.

GETTING AROUND LONDON

Walking

London is a great walking city. Sure it's busy and bustling but precincts are close together (i.e. Soho and Covent Garden or Knightsbridge and South Kensington) and walking allows you time to admire the grandeur or simply stroll through an elegant park. If you want company, Eating Europe (www.eatingeurope.com) and Context Travel (www.contexttravel.com) offer immersive tours on foot.

London has a great public transport system with plenty of options. See **Transport for London**: www.tfl.gov.uk for maps and more information, but here are the basics.

Tickets (Oyster cards)

Visitor Oyster cards, which can be purchased online before you travel, are plastic smartcards instead of paper tickets. It is the cheapest way to pay for single journeys on bus, Tube, tram, DLR, London Overground and other rail services in London. They're rechargeable and you can buy zoned daily or weekly tickets on them. Simply tap the Oyster card as you go through Tube station ticket gates and when you leave stations and it will calculate your fare. Be mindful of tapping off or your card will automatically incur a fine. On buses you only need to tap by the driver when you board – not when you leave.

Tube

The London Underground train system, or Tube, operates in central and greater London, and connects with various smaller lines and the Overground, in outer London, for full network coverage. Keep a Tube map handy at all times (they're available at stations) to navigate the 11 colour-coded main lines. Knowing whether you're heading southbound or northbound is key to navigating your way around. Services run from 5am to 12.30am on most routes. Night Tube services run on the Jubilee, Victoria, Piccadilly and most of the Central and Northern lines all night on Fridays and Saturdays.

When travelling by Tube, note that many stations are deep underground and require long escalator rides where you should always stand on the right unless overtaking on the left. Only some stations have lifts – marked as accessible on the Tube map. Courtesy and crowds dictate that you allow passengers off trains before boarding (stand to the side of the doors). Don't panic if you miss a train (or it's too crowded to get on), as most lines have trains operating every couple of minutes and the wait times are clearly shown at each station's platform. Be practical when travelling by Tube and carry a bottle of water – especially in summer as trains can get hot.

Bus

Taking the iconic red double-decker buses around London is a great way to get your bearings in the city and see the sights. Buses run from 5am to 12.30am. Night buses operate on many major routes from midnight to 5am, and some operate a 24-hour service. You cannot pay your bus fare in cash, you have to have an Oyster card (*see* p. 156). If you want to ride up top, hang onto the stair rail as you climb as buses pull out suddenly.

Taxi

It feels very 'London' taking a black cab. These gorgeous old-fashioned cars with drivers who take pride in their work can be hailed on the street when the yellow light is on. Payment is usually in cash, but credit cards are becoming more prevalent.

Mini cabs are the budget version, they're plain cars that can be booked by phone or app. Note that there are many mini cab operators and it's best to choose a reputable or recommended one.

Uber cars (www.uber.com) are also available.

Water taxi

The **Thames Clipper** (www.thamesclippers. com) service is becoming more popular giving commuters and tourists the opportunity to travel up and down the river between Putney and North Greenwich. A 'river roamer' ticket enables you to hop on and off at 17 piers, including London Eye (Waterloo), Westminster and Tower of London and Greenwich. It's a lovely way to see the city.

Cycling

Santander Cycles (www.tfl.gov.uk/ modes/cycling/santander-cycles) or Boris bikes (after the mayor that introduced them) are popular hire bikes. There are more than 11,500 bikes that you can ride on short trips between 750 docking stations around London, using your credit card for access. If you're unfamiliar cycling in a big city, London traffic can be chaotic (although often slow-moving because of congestion). Remember: Don't ride through red traffic lights – you'll risk your life and a £50 fine; don't cycle on the pavement or up a one-way street (unless clearly marked for cyclists); use appropriate hand signals to indicate that you're turning left or right; don't use a mobile phone or earphones; and consider wearing a helmet (they're not obligatory in the UK).

Driving

International visitors can drive any small vehicle (car or motorcycle) with a full and valid licence for 12 months after entry to Great Britain. You will need your driving licence, proof of address and your passport to pick up a hire car (reputable companies include: Avis, Hertz and Budget). Check that insurance cover is included. You will also require a credit card for a deposit. Drivers under 25 might incur additional charges.

Driving tips:

* Always overtake on the right-hand side (the driver's side) and use the left lane to drive in.
* Speed limits range from 20–40mph (50–65km/h) in built-up areas and a maximum of 70mph (110km/h) on motorways or dual carriageways.
* Wearing seatbelts is compulsory and fines can be incurred for not using them.
* Central London has a London Congestion Charge, applicable weekdays between 7am and 6pm (excluding public holidays) at a cost of £11.50 per day. You can register online at www.tfl.gov.uk. Ignoring the charge results in hefty fines.
* Avoid peak hour traffic on weekdays between 8–9.30am and 5–7pm when people are travelling to/from work/schools.
* Central London parking restrictions are hard to avoid. Don't park on double red or yellow lines; single lines sometimes mean you can park in the evenings and at weekends, but check road-side signs carefully for restrictions. Keep a supply of coins handy for parking meters.
* British drivers flash their headlights to either indicate that they are stopping to let you pass, or to say thank you if you let them in.

TIME ZONES

From November to March, Britain is on Greenwich Mean Time (GMT). From late March until late October, the clocks go forward one hour to British Summer Time (BST).

MEDIA & TOURIST INFO

Time Out, www.timeout.com/london – a listicle down-low of the city's newest and best eats, drinks and activities

www.londonist.com – a collation of articles, events and what's new in London

www.visitlondon.com – official London visitor guide and ticket sales

www.theculturetrip.com – a curation of London's arts, culture, food & drink

Visit Britain, www.visitbritain.com – official Britain visitor guide.

If you're interested in seeing multiple historic sites, palaces, castles or gardens around Britain, both **English Heritage** (www.english-heritage.org.uk) and **National Trust** (www.nationaltrust.org.uk) offer overseas visitor passes.

CLIMATE

The UK is known for its below average weather and an Englishman without his umbrella is a rarity indeed. That's the joke anyway. But indeed, the UK is influenced by the Atlantic ocean and rain, cloudiness and cool temperatures are more common than sunshine. The good news is that the climate is a bit milder in London than in the rest of Britain with an average maximum temperature of 23°C (73°F) in summer and 8°C (46°F) in winter.

WI-FI

You can find wi-fi in cafes, bars, pubs, hotel foyers and, increasingly, galleries and tourist attractions. It is mostly free when you're sitting down and using your laptop, tablet or phone, but ordering something is generally considered polite.

LGBTIQ

There's a lot going on for the LGBTIQ community in London. Most of the media and tourist websites listed above have info on LGBT (as it is mostly referred in the UK) -friendly hotels, gay bars and special events. Of course, the best time to be in London is in July for Pride (prideinlondon. org), when Soho takes on even more of a festival atmosphere. And it's worth checking out Brighton (see p. 138). It's the self-styled gay capital of Britain.

OPENING HOURS

Retail stores are generally open seven days a week between 10am and 5.30pm, with some of the bigger stores and department stores staying open until 7pm. Speciality and boutique stores in the centre of London often have one day a week when they'll be open late. Check market timetables as some have late-night shopping.

In general, restaurants and cafes will serve breakfast between 7am and 11pm, lunch between 12pm and 2.30pm and dinner between 6pm and 9/10pm but many kitchens will stay open all day. Bars generally shut their doors between 11pm and 1am, but like all big cities you can find late-night clubs and bars to keep you going all night, especially given London now has 24-hour Tube options.

SUMMER PEAK SEASON

If you like crowds and good times, the UK summer from June to August is the best time to be in London. All the weather-reliant major events and festivals are on and shops and businesses tend to extend hours and services. On the downside, this is peak tourist season and the UK's major school holiday period, so expect longer queues and more expensive accommodation.

POSTCODES & GPS

Introduced during World War I, London's postcodes don't make a tonne of sense. The system identifies a 'central' district with north, south, south-east, west etc indicated by N1, S1, SE1, W1 and so on. The numbers then follow alphabetical order rather than geographical order – SW7 is South Kensington, SW8 is South Lambeth and SW9 is Stockwell (which includes Brixton). To be clear, these suburbs aren't neighbours. On the upside, the full residential postcodes – containing six letters and numbers (ie NW1 6GB) relate to small areas of only 10–15 addresses. They're key to navigating London if you're driving with a GPS: tapping the postcode in will get you there.

VOLTAGE & CONVERTERS

UK appliances are fitted with plugs that have three rectangular pins. The power sockets deliver an average voltage of 220/240 AC, 50 Hz. Only appliances built for 220–240 volts should use these plugs. Converters are available from department stores, souvenir shops and petrol (gas) stations. The two-pronged European style sockets in hotel bathrooms are for shavers only. Hotel bathrooms tend not to have powerpoints.

WEIGHTS & MEASURES

Britain is officially metric, yes? Correct. Britain, like Europe, has adopted the metric system, but some imperial measures are still in use, especially for road distances, which are measured in miles. And to confuse you more, imperial pints and gallons are 20 per cent larger than US measures.

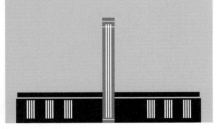

EATING & DRINKING IN LONDON

Reservations

While it is standard at many restaurants to reserve a table, the first-come first-served theory is on-trend at niche little eateries where seats are few and service is faster than usual. Some restaurants have apps that will tell you when your table is up.

Halal

With a large Islamic community and an annual Halal Food Festival in August each year, there's no shortage of Halal food in London, both in traditional Middle Eastern cuisines and mainstream restaurants.

Vegetarian, vegan, gluten-free

It's not hard to track down vegan and vegetarian restaurants with food that ticks the full-flavour boxes. In addition, menus in restaurants city-wide have adopted the little symbols that allow diners to avoid or choose different dishes depending on their 'dietaries'.

Tipping

Workers do not rely on tips in the UK, they are paid the minimum wage. That said, London restaurants almost always add a 12.5% 'discretionary tip' onto the bill. When they don't, it is customary to round-up to the nearest £10, especially if you've enjoyed the service. Similarly, giving a gold nugget or two to hotel staff and taxi drivers is good karma all round. When it doubt, add 10%.

Discretionary donation

It's becoming a thing for restaurants to add a discretionary donation on top of the discretionary tip. It's usually 1% of the total bill and it goes to a cause close to the heart of the restaurant.

FESTIVALS

There are too many to list, obviously, and most of them happen in July when the sun is more likely to be shining. Try these on for size:

British Summer Time Hyde (bst-hydepark.com) – a family friendly festival with live bands held in July at Hyde Park.

Pride (prideinlondon.org) – the much-loved LGBTIQ festival held across the city in July each year.

South West Four (southwestfour.com) – or SW4 is a DJ-heavy music fest for dancers on Clapham Common in August.

Wireless (wirelessfestival.co.uk) – North London's biggest music event attracting 10,000 people. At Finsbury park over a weekend in July.

Notting Hill Carnival (www.thelondonnottinghillcarnival.com) – a two-day late August extravanganza with Caribbean heritage at it roots.

PHONES

International visitors wanting to use their smartphones can purchase prepaid SIM cards from supermarkets, kiosks, drug stores and official outlets, as well as all international airports. The UK network uses the 900 or 1800 GSM system. US visitors (where the system is 800 or 1900 MHz band) wanting to use their own handset will need to acquire a tri- or quad-band set.

Britain's international dialling code is +44 (0044). If calling a landline to London from overseas, include the regional dialling code (0). Note that the 0 is removed from the phone number and prefix if used in conjunction with an additional code.

Britain's little red public phone boxes are often used to house emergency defibrillators nowadays, but many of them still have good old fashioned telephones. You can use phonecards, credit cards or coins.

MONEY & ATMS

The pound sterling is the currency and the symbol is £ for pound and p for pence. The pound comes in notes of £50, £20, £10, £5 and pence comes in coins of 1p, 2p, 5p, 10p, 20p, 50p

You'll find ATMs in post offices, banks, supermarkets, petrol (gas) stations, train stations, Tube stations etc. As a general rule, most vendors accept card payments. You'll find 'wave and pay' and 'tap and go' contactless cards in most places, too. In some stores if you use an overseas credit card, they'll ask to see your passport or driver's licence.

EMBASSY CONTACTS

Australian Embassy
Australia House, Strand, WC2B 4LA
020 7887 5776 (9am–4.30pm weekdays)
+61 2 6261 3305 (all other times)
consular.lhlh@dfat.gov.au
uk.embassy.gov.au

NZ Embassy
80 Haymarket, SW1Y 4TQ
020 7930 8422 Mon–Fri 9am–5pm
www.mfat.govt.nz

US Embassy
33 Nine Elms Lane, SW11 7US
020 7499 9000
uk.usembassy.gov

Canadian Embassy
Canada House, Trafalgar Square, SW1Y 5BJ
020 7004 6000
ldn.consular@international.gc.ca
www.unitedkingdon.gc.ca

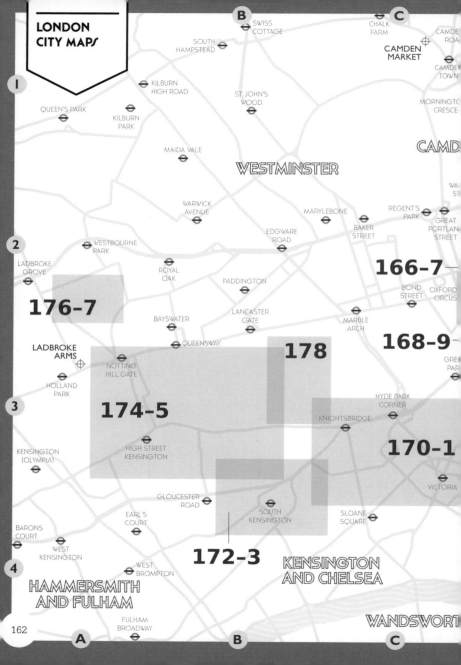

I

QUEEN'S PARK

KILBURN
PARK

KILBURN
HIGH ROAD

SOUTH
HAMPSTEAD

B SWISS
COTTAGE

ST JOHN'S
WOOD

CHALK
FARM

C

CAMDE
ROA

CAMDEN
MARKET

CAMDE
TOWN

MORNINGTO
CRESCE

MAIDA VALE

WESTMINSTER

CAMD

WARWICK
AVENUE

MARYLEBONE

REGENT'S
PARK

BAKER
STREET

WA
S'

GREAT
PORTLAN
STREET

EDGWARE
ROAD

2

WESTBOURNE
PARK

LADBROKE
GROVE

166-7

ROYAL
OAK

PADDINGTON

BOND
STREET

OXFORD
CIRCUS

176-7

BAYSWATER

LANCASTER
GATE

MARBLE
ARCH

168-9

QUEENSWAY

178

GRE
PAR

LADBROKE
ARMS

NOTTING
HILL GATE

HOLLAND
PARK

HYDE PARK
CORNER

3

174-5

KNIGHTSBRIDGE

170-1

KENSINGTON
(OLYMPIA)

HIGH STREET
KENSINGTON

VICTORIA

GLOUCESTER
ROAD

SOUTH
KENSINGTON

SLOANE
SQUARE

BARONS
COURT

EARL'S
COURT

WEST
KENSINGTON

WEST
BROMPTON

172-3

KENSINGTON
AND CHELSEA

4

HAMMERSMITH
AND FULHAM

FULHAM
BROADWAY

WANDSWORT

A

B

C

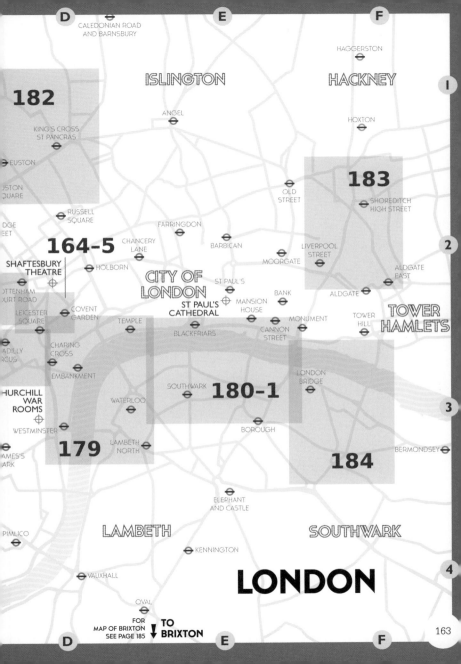

D

CALEDONIAN ROAD
AND BARNSBURY

E

HAGGERSTON

F

I

ISLINGTON

HACKNEY

182

ANGEL

HOXTON

KING'S CROSS
ST PANCRAS

EUSTON

USTON
QUARE

RUSSELL
SQUARE

OLD
STREET

183

SHOREDITCH
HIGH STREET

DGE
EET

164-5

FARRINGDON

CHANCERY
LANE

BARBICAN

LIVERPOOL
STREET

SHAFTESBURY
THEATRE

HOLBORN

MOORGATE

ALDGATE
EAST

OTTENHAM
URT ROAD

CITY OF
LONDON

ST PAUL'S

BANK

ALDGATE

2

LEICESTER
SQUARE

COVENT
GARDEN

TEMPLE

ST PAUL'S
CATHEDRAL

MANSION
HOUSE

MONUMENT

TOWER
HILL

TOWER
HAMLETS

ADILLY
RCUS

CHARING
CROSS

BLACKFRIARS

CANNON
STREET

CHURCHILL
WAR
ROOMS

EMBANKMENT

SOUTHWARK

180-1

LONDON
BRIDGE

WATERLOO

WESTMINSTER

LAMBETH
NORTH

BOROUGH

AMES'S
ARK

179

BERMONDSEY

184

PIMLICO

ELEPHANT
AND CASTLE

LAMBETH

SOUTHWARK

KENNINGTON

LONDON

VAUXHALL

3

4

OVAL

FOR
MAP OF BRIXTON
SEE PAGE 185

**TO
BRIXTON**

D

E

F

163

SOHO SQUARE

A

B

C

BATEMAN'S BUILDINGS

GREEK STREET

MANETTE STREET

CHARING CROSS ROAD

FLITCROFT STREET

NEW COMPTON STREET

I

SOHO

Foyles

PHOENIX STREET

STACEY STREET

The Phoenix Garden

ODEON Covent Garden (cinema)

FRITH STREET

BATEMAN STREET

CAMDEN

MERCER

SHAFTESBURY

AVE

SUPER SUPERFICIAL

2

HOPPERS

GREEK STREET

STREET

EARLHAM ST

TOWER STREET

COMPTON STREET

SHAFTESBURY AVENUE

FABRIQUE ARTISAN BAKERY

Tristan Bates Theatre

WEST STREET

OLD

Palace Theatre

CHARING

TOWER STREET

St Mary Theat

FRITH STREET

Curzon Soho (cinema)

AVENUE

LITCHFIELD STREET

3

ROMILLY

SHAFTESBURY

GERRARD PLACE

CROSS

ROAD

MACCLESFIELD STREET

STREET

NEWPORT COURT

GREAT NEWPORT

DANSEY PLACE

GERRARD STREET

LITTLE NEWPORT STREET

4

OPIUM

STREET

Prince Charles Cinema

LEICESTER COURT

LEICESTER SQUARE

LISLE

Leicester Square Theatre

Vue (cinema)

164

A

B

C

D

E

F

NEAL STREET

BETTERTON STREET

SHELTON STREET

ARNE STREET

STREET

1

vent
rden
el

NEAL'S YARD

HOMESLICE

GARDENS

NOTTINGHAM COURT

NEAL

ENDELL

STREET

0   50 m

MONMOUTH STREET

SHORTS

CUCUMBER ALLEY

STREET

N

Radisson Blu
Edwardian

THE
ESCAPOLOGIST

STREET

NEAL

HANOVER PLACE

Seven
Dials
Sundial
Pillar

EARLHAM

Cambridge
Theatre

ROCOCO
CHOCOLATES

STREET

STREET

LONG   ACRE

2

MERCER STREET

SHELTON

LANGLEY

COVENT
GARDEN

JAMES

Ching Court

MERCER

MERCER

WALK

STREET

LONG

COVENT
GARDEN

ROYAL
OPERA
HOUSE
(ENTRANCE ON
BOW STREET)

TATTY
DEVINE

PLACE

STANFORDS

ACRE

LANGLEY COURT

STREET

3

SLINGSBY

St Martin's
Courtyard

SLINGSBY PLACE

LONG

BANBURY COURT

FLORAL

STREET

CONDUIT COURT

WESTMINSTER

COVENT
GARDEN
MARKET

GARRICK

Floral Court

KING

STREET

ST PAUL'S
CHURCH

4

STREET

NEW   ROW

HENRIETTA STREET

D

E

F

A B C

GREAT

MARGARET STREET

MARGARET STREET

FITZROVIA

STREET

Lond
Editi
(hot

BERNER

EASTCASTLE

WELLS

WINSLEY

ADAM AND EVE COURT

STREET

PORTLAND

GREAT

CASTLE STREET

STREET

PLACE

STREET

MARKET

OXFORD STREET

BE

WESTMINSTER

POLAND STREET

OXFORD
CIRCUS

HILLS PLACE

RAMILLIES PLACE

RAMILLIES

N

NOEL

STREET

STREET

POLAND

LITTLE ARGYLL STREET

ARGYLL STREET

London
Palladium

MARLBOROUGH

PHONICA
RECORDS

D'ARBLA

GREAT

0   50 m

Liberty
London

PLACE

NEWBURGH STREET

MARSHALL

STREET

KINGLY

REGENT

STREET

FOUBERT'S

STREET

BROADWICK

STREET

BAO

**CARNABY
STREET**

KINGLY

CONDUIT STREET

GANTON STREET

KINGLY COURT

SPIRIT OF
SOHO

STREET

BRIDLE LANE

STREET

TENISON
COURT

KINGLY COURT

BEAK

A B C

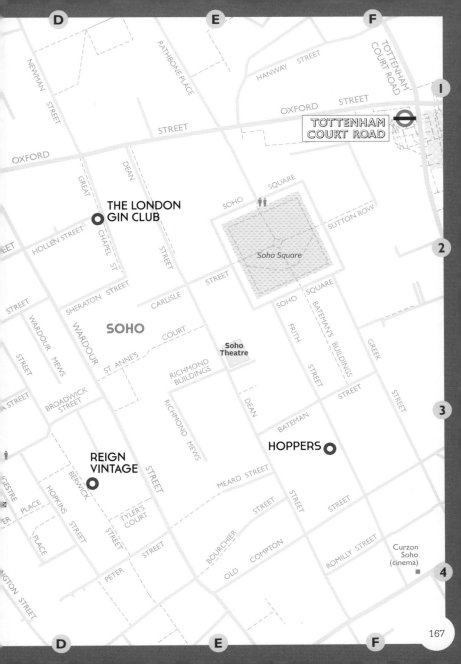

D

E

F

NEWMAN STREET

RATHBONE PLACE

HANWAY STREET

TOTTENHAM COURT ROAD

I

OXFORD STREET

STREET

TOTTENHAM COURT ROAD

OXFORD

DEAN

SOHO SQUARE

GREAT

○ THE LONDON GIN CLUB

CHAPEL ST

SUTTON ROW

HOLLEN STREET

STREET

2

Soho Square

SOHO SQUARE

EET

STREET

CARLISLE

STREET

SHERATON STREET

FRITH

BATEMAN'S BUILDINGS

GREEK

WARDOUR MEWS

SOHO

COURT

STREET

STREET

STREET

WARDOUR

ST ANNE'S

Soho Theatre

RICHMOND BUILDINGS

STREET

BROADWICK STREET

A STREET

RICHMOND MEWS

DEAN

BATEMAN

3

HOPPERS ○

REIGN VINTAGE ○

BERWICK

STREET

MEARD STREET

STREET

STREET

STREET

HOPKINS STREET

PLACE

ER

TYLER'S COURT

STREET

BOURCHIER

STREET

ROMILLY STREET

Curzon Soho (cinema)

PLACE

STREET

PETER

OLD COMPTON

4

GTON STREET

NGTON STREET

167

D

E

F

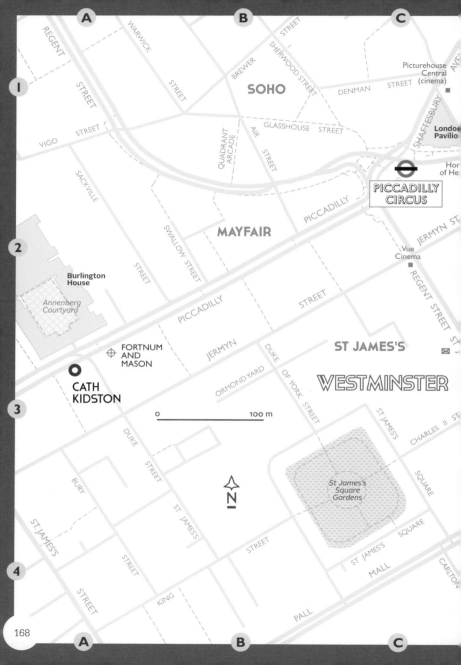

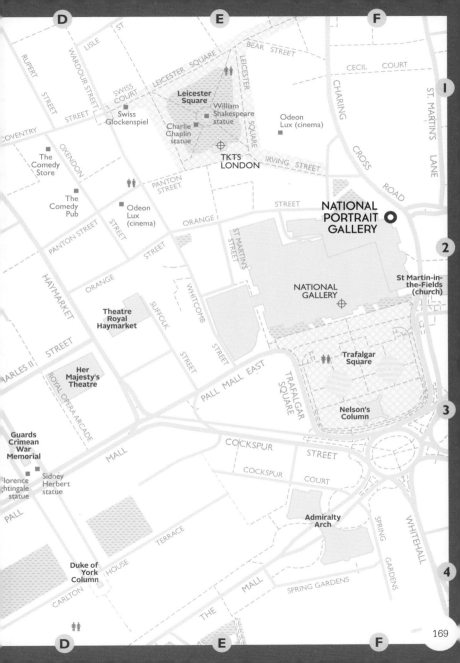

D **E** **F**

I

ST

LISLE ST

WARDOUR STREET

RUPERT STREET

LEICESTER SQUARE

BEAR STREET

CECIL COURT

CHARING CROSS ROAD

ST MARTIN'S LANE

SWISS COURT

Leicester Square

Swiss Glockenspiel

William Shakespeare statue

Charlie Chaplin statue

Odeon Lux (cinema)

LEICESTER SQUARE

COVENTRY STREET

OXENDON STREET

The Comedy Store

PANTON STREET

⊕ TKTS LONDON

IRVING STREET

The Comedy Pub

Odeon Lux (cinema)

STREET

ORANGE STREET

NATIONAL PORTRAIT GALLERY ⭕

PANTON STREET

STREET

ST MARTIN'S STREET

2

HAYMARKET

ORANGE STREET

WHITCOMB STREET

NATIONAL GALLERY ⊕

St Martin-in-the-Fields (church)

Theatre Royal Haymarket

SUFFOLK STREET

Her Majesty's Theatre

ROYAL OPERA ARCADE

STREET

PALL MALL EAST

TRAFALGAR SQUARE

Trafalgar Square

Nelson's Column

3

CHARLES II STREET

COCKSPUR STREET

Guards Crimean War Memorial

MALL

COCKSPUR COURT

Florence Nightingale statue

Sidney Herbert statue

SPRING GARDENS

WHITEHALL

PALL

CARLTON HOUSE TERRACE

Admiralty Arch

4

Duke of York Column

THE MALL

SPRING GARDENS

CARLTON

D **E** **F**

Apsley
House

Bomber
Command
Memorial

GREEN   PARK

WELLINGTON
ARCH

DE PARK
ORNER

Memorial
Gates

CONSTITUTION   HILL

Australian
War Memorial

BUCKINGHAM
PALACE

STREET

HEADFORT PLACE

GROSVENOR

MONTROSE PLACE

CHAPEL

STREET

Buckingham Palace Gardens

N

0   100 m

The Queen's
Gallery

JARE

CHESTER

CHESTER MEWS   STREET

PLACE

WESTMINSTER

The
Royal
Mews

UPPER   BELGRAVE

WILTON

BELGRAVE

ECCLESTON MEWS

SQUARE

STREET

Grosvenor
Gardens

GROSVENOR

BEESTON PLACE

BUCKINGHAM   PALACE   ROAD

NORTH

PLACE

SQUARE

LOWER BELGRAVE STREET

GARDENS

VICTORIA

EATON

ECCLESTON

STREET

Little Ben
Miniature
clock tower

Eaton
Square
Gardens

EATON

EATON MEWS SOUTH

SQUARE

STREET

BELGRAVIA

EBURY

BUCKINGHAM PALACE ROAD

LONDON
VICTORIA

WILTON   ROAD

ELIZABETH STREET

CHESTER

EBURY MEWS

EBURY STREET

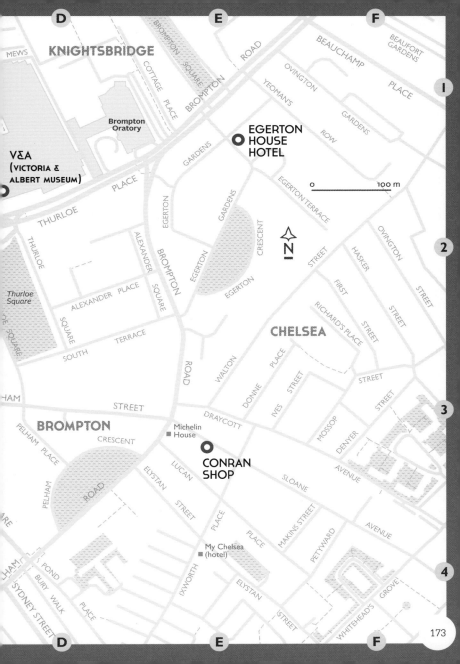

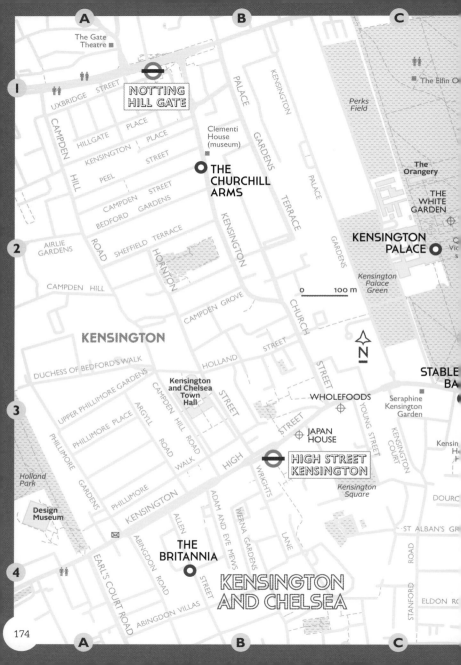

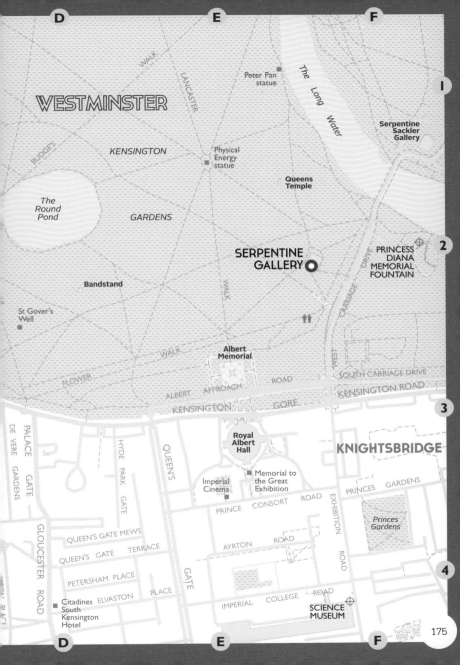

WESTMINSTER

KENSINGTON

GARDENS

The Round Pond

Peter Pan statue

The Long Water

Serpentine Sackler Gallery

Physical Energy statue

Queens Temple

SERPENTINE GALLERY

PRINCESS DIANA MEMORIAL FOUNTAIN

Bandstand

St Gover's Well

Albert Memorial

FLOWER WALK

ALBERT APPROACH ROAD

KENSINGTON GORE

KENSINGTON ROAD

SOUTH CARRIAGE DRIVE

CARRIAGE DRIVE

WEST

PALACE GATE

DE VERE GARDENS

HYDE PARK GATE

QUEEN'S GATE

Royal Albert Hall

KNIGHTSBRIDGE

Imperial Cinema

Memorial to the Great Exhibition

PRINCES GARDENS

PRINCE CONSORT ROAD

Princes Gardens

EXHIBITION ROAD

GLOUCESTER ROAD

QUEEN'S GATE MEWS

QUEEN'S GATE TERRACE

AYRTON ROAD

PETERSHAM PLACE

ELVASTON PLACE

GATE

Citadines South Kensington Hotel

IMPERIAL COLLEGE ROAD

SCIENCE MUSEUM

BUDGES

LANCASTER WALK

WALK

WALK

175

D E F

D E F I

1 2 3 4

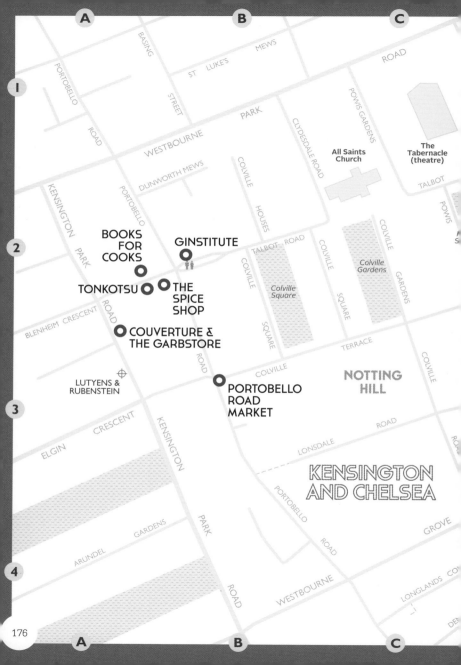

A

B

C

1

BASING

STREET

ST LUKES MEWS

PARK

WESTBOURNE

PORTOBELLO

ROAD

KENSINGTON

PORTOBELLO

DUNWORTH MEWS

CLYDESDALE ROAD

POWIS GARDENS

All Saints
Church

The
Tabernacle
(theatre)

ROAD

TALBOT

POWIS

COLVILLE HOUSES

2

PARK

**BOOKS
FOR
COOKS** ●

GINSTITUTE ●

TALBOT ROAD

COLVILLE

COLVILLE SQUARE

COLVILLE GARDENS

*Colville
Gardens*

*Colville
Square*

TONKOTSU ● ● **THE
SPICE
SHOP**

ROAD

BLENHEIM CRESCENT

● **COUVERTURE &
THE GARBSTORE**

SQUARE

TERRACE

⊕
LUTYENS &
RUBENSTEIN

ROAD

COLVILLE

● **PORTOBELLO
ROAD
MARKET**

**NOTTING
HILL**

COLVILLE

3

ELGIN

CRESCENT

KENSINGTON

LONSDALE

ROAD

PORTOBELLO

**KENSINGTON
AND CHELSEA**

ROAD

PARK

GARDENS

ARUNDEL

GROVE

4

ROAD

WESTBOURNE

LONGLANDS

176

A

B

C

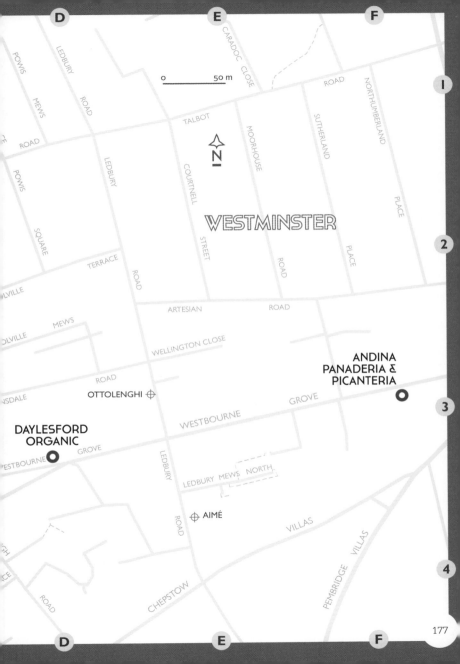

D

E

F

POWIS

LEDBURY

CARADOC CLOSE

ROAD

NORTHUMBERLAND

MEWS

ROAD

0   50 m

TALBOT

SUTHERLAND

ROAD

LEDBURY

MOORHOUSE

N

POWIS

COURTNELL

PLACE

WESTMINSTER

SQUARE

STREET

ROAD

PLACE

TERRACE

ROAD

LVILLE

ARTESIAN   ROAD

LVILLE   MEWS

WELLINGTON CLOSE

NSDALE

ROAD

OTTOLENGHI ⊕

**ANDINA
PANADERIA &
PICANTERIA**

O

GROVE

**DAYLESFORD
ORGANIC**

WESTBOURNE

ESTBOURNE O   GROVE

LEDBURY

LEDBURY MEWS NORTH

ROAD

⊕ AIMÉ

VILLAS

HIGH

PEMBRIDGE VILLAS

VILLAS

ICE

ROAD

CHEPSTOW

D

E

F

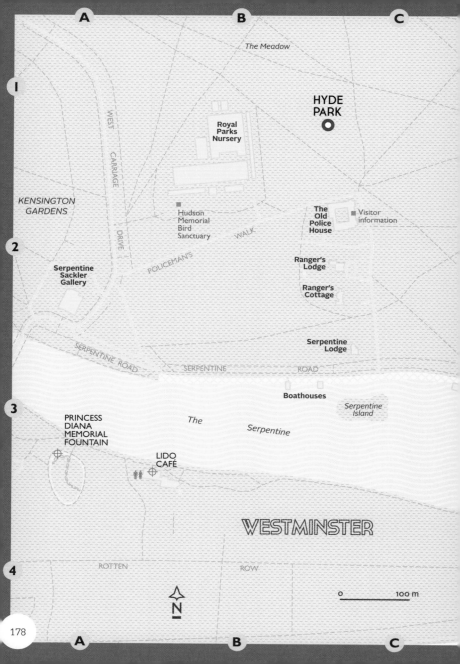

A
B
C

I

The Meadow

HYDE
PARK

WEST

CARRIAGE

Royal
Parks
Nursery

KENSINGTON
GARDENS

Hudson
Memorial
Bird
Sanctuary

DRIVE

WALK

The
Old
Police
House

Visitor
information

2

POLICEMAN'S

Serpentine
Sackler
Gallery

Ranger's
Lodge

Ranger's
Cottage

SERPENTINE ROAD

Serpentine
Lodge

SERPENTINE

ROAD

Boathouses

Serpentine
Island

3

PRINCESS
DIANA
MEMORIAL
FOUNTAIN

The

Serpentine

LIDO
CAFÉ

WESTMINSTER

4

ROTTEN

ROW

N

0   100 m

A
B
C

A

ST PAUL'S CHURCH
LONDON TRANSPORT MUSEUM
Henrietta Hotel
MAIDEN LANE
STRAND
BEDFORD STREET

WESTMINSTER

SAVOY
STRAND
PLACE

CHARING CROSS

Victoria Embankment Gardens

EMBANKMENT

NORTHUMBERLAND AVENUE

WHITEHALL PLACE

Whitehall Gardens

Royal Horseguards Hotel

Whitehall Gardens

WHITEHALL

RICHMOND TERRACE

PARLIAMENT STREET

WESTMINSTER

Parliament Square

BIG BEN

Palace of Westminster

HOUSES OF PARLIAMENT

Westminster Abbey

Abingdon Street Gardens

B

SOMERSET HOUSE

LANCASTER PL

VICTORIA EMBANKMENT

N

WATERLOO BRIDGE

FESTIVAL

EMBANKMENT

WAHACA
Queen Elizabeth Hall
Royal Festival Hall
Hayward Gallery

South Bank Book Market

SOUTH BANK PROMENADE

Jubilee Gardens

LONDON EYE-WATERLOO

LONDON EYE

Premier Inn

The London Dungeon
County Hall

London Aquarium

London Marriot Hotel

WESTMINSTER MILLENNIUM

Thames

WESTMINSTER

WESTMINSTER BRIDGE

The Florence Nightingale Museum

River

LAMBETH

BELVEDERE ROAD

YORK ROAD

LAMBETH

PALACE RD

Archbishop's Park

C

SURREY ST
EMBANKMENT
Temple Stairs Arch

River Thames

0   100 m

Olivier Theatre
Dorfman Theatre
Lyttelton Theatre
National Theatre

UPPER GROUND

SOUTH BANK

STAMFORD ST

Imax BFI

WATERLOO

LONDON WATERLOO

Leake St graffiti tunnel

Park Plaza

The Vaults (theatre)

House of Vans skatepark

THE TRAVEL CAFE
Point A Hotel London

LAMBETH NORTH

179

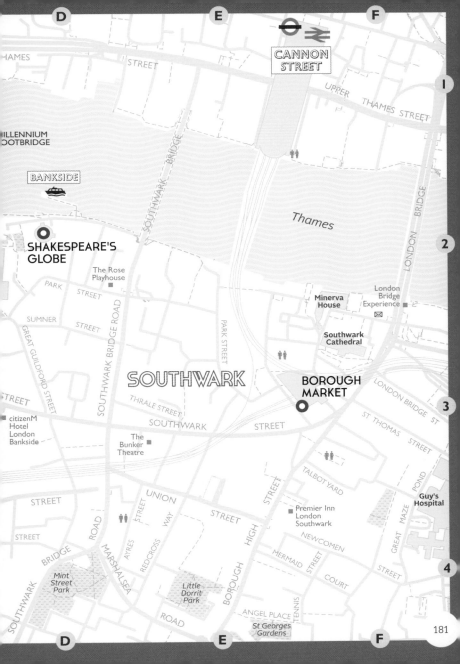

D **E** **F**

CANNON STREET

I

UPPER THAMES STREET

MILLENNIUM FOOTBRIDGE

SOUTHWARK BRIDGE

STREET

Thames

LONDON BRIDGE

2

BANKSIDE

SHAKESPEARE'S GLOBE

The Rose Playhouse

PARK STREET

SUMNER STREET

GREAT GUILFORD STREET

SOUTHWARK BRIDGE ROAD

PARK STREET

Minerva House

London Bridge Experience

Southwark Cathedral

SOUTHWARK

BOROUGH MARKET

LONDON BRIDGE ST

ST THOMAS STREET

3

citizenM Hotel London Bankside

THRALE STREET

SOUTHWARK STREET

The Bunker Theatre

TALBOT YARD

STREET

Premier Inn London Southwark

NEWCOMEN STREET

GREAT MAZE POND

Guy's Hospital

STREET

UNION STREET

STREET

REDCROSS WAY

AYRES STREET

STREET

MARSHALSEA ROAD

Mint Street Park

BOROUGH HIGH STREET

MERMAID STREET

COURT

STREET

4

SOUTHWARK BRIDGE ROAD

Little Dorrit Park

ANGEL PLACE

St Georges Gardens

TENNIS STREET

D **E** **F**

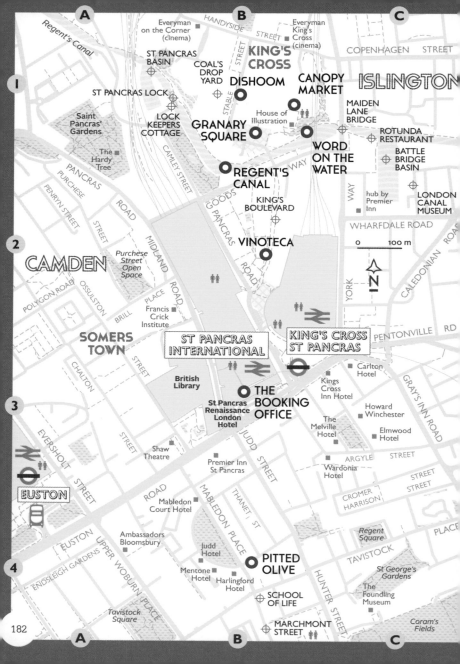

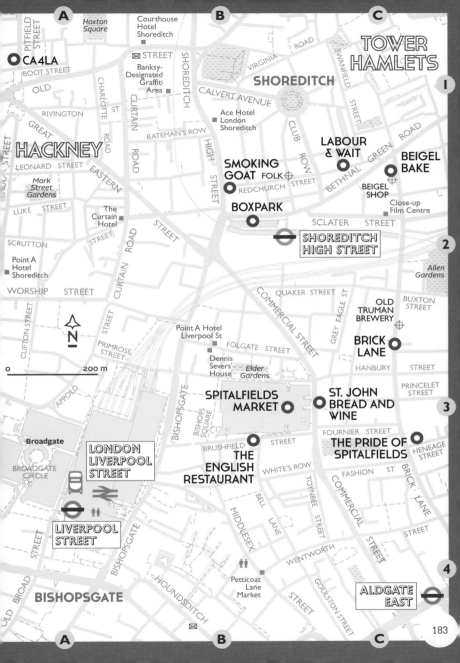

A
- PITFIELD STREET
- Hoxton Square
- CA4LA
- BOOT STREET
- OLD
- RIVINGTON
- GREAT EASTERN STREET
- HACKNEY
- LEONARD STREET
- CHARLOTTE ST
- Mark Street Gardens
- LUKE STREET
- The Curtain Hotel
- SCRUTTON STREET
- Point A Hotel Shoreditch
- WORSHIP STREET
- CLIFTON STREET
- N
- 0   200 m
- PRIMROSE STREET
- APPOLD
- Broadgate
- BROADGATE CIRCLE
- OLD BROAD STREET
- LIVERPOOL STREET

B
- Courthouse Hotel Shoreditch
- STREET
- Banksy-Designated Graffiti Area
- SHOREDITCH HIGH STREET
- CALVERT AVENUE
- BATEMAN'S ROW
- Ace Hotel London Shoreditch
- SMOKING GOAT
- FOLK
- REDCHURCH STREET
- BOXPARK
- CURTAIN ROAD
- SHOREDITCH HIGH STREET
- COMMERCIAL STREET
- QUAKER STREET
- Point A Hotel Liverpool St
- FOLGATE STREET
- Dennis Severs' House
- Elder Gardens
- BISHOPSGATE
- SPITALFIELDS MARKET
- BISHOPS SQUARE
- BRUSHFIELD STREET
- THE ENGLISH RESTAURANT
- WHITE'S ROW
- LONDON LIVERPOOL STREET
- LIVERPOOL STREET
- BELL LANE
- MIDDLESEX STREET
- HOUNDSDITCH
- BISHOPSGATE
- Petticoat Lane Market
- WENTWORTH
- BISHOPSGATE

C
- ROAD
- SWANFIELD STREET
- TOWER HAMLETS
- VIRGINIA ROAD
- SHOREDITCH
- CLUB ROW
- BETHNAL GREEN ROAD
- LABOUR & WAIT
- BEIGEL BAKE
- BEIGEL SHOP
- Close-up Film Centre
- SCLATER STREET
- Allen Gardens
- BUXTON STREET
- OLD TRUMAN BREWERY
- GREY EAGLE ST
- BRICK LANE
- HANBURY STREET
- ST. JOHN BREAD AND WINE
- PRINCELET STREET
- FOURNIER STREET
- THE PRIDE OF SPITALFIELDS
- HENEAGE STREET
- FASHION ST
- BRICK LANE
- TOYNBEE STREET
- COMMERCIAL STREET
- GOULSTON STREET
- ALDGATE EAST

A

B

C

1

LOWER THAMES STREET

👥

Crown
Jewels

**TOWER OF
LONDON**

👥👥

River

🚤

**LONDON
BRIDGE CITY**

**HMS
Belfast**

🚤

**TOWER
MILLENNIUM**

St Katharines Way

The
Tower-
Guoman
Hotels

👥

**Hay's
Galleria**

Thames

**TOWER
BRIDGE** ◎

🚤

**LONDON
BRIDGE**

🚊
🚇🚅

👥👥 👥

MORE LONDON PLACE

👥

**City
Hall**

👥👥

**Tower
Bridge
Engine
Room**

**SAINT
KATHARINE**

◎
**THE
SHARD**

TOOLEY

Bridge
Theatre

SHAD

THAMES

Shangri-La
Hotel

ST THOMAS

*Potters
Fields
Park*

BRIDGE ROAD

2

**Guy's
Hospital**

STREET

STREET

BERMONDSEY

SNOWSFIELDS

WESTON

STREET

St John's
Churchyard

TOOLEY

QUEEN

ELIZABETH

STREET

*Guy
Street
Park*

KIPLING

KIRBY GROVE

BERMONDSEY

Whites
Grounds
Skatepark

TOWER

STREET

CURLEW

STREET

DRUID
STREET

3

*Leathermarket
Gardens*

**JOSÉ
TAPAS
BAR** ◎

✛ **FASHION &
TEXTILE
MUSEUM**

**MALTBY
STREET
MARKET**

LEATHERMARKET ST.

TANNER

✛

*Tanner
Street
Park*

STREET

**40
MALTBY
STREET** ◎
◎

DRUID ST.

LONG LANE

WESTON STREET

MOROCCO ST.

TANNER STREET

✛

Premier Inn
London
Tower
Bridge

TOWER BRIDGE ROAD

MALTBY STREET

ROPE
WALK

**WHITE
CUBE
GALLERY**

MANCIPLE STREET

WESTON LANE

Residence Inn
Marriott

PIZARRO

✛
*Saint Mary
Magdalen
Churchyard*

ABBEY

STREET

**FLOUR &
GRAPE** ◎◎

THE GRANGE

GRANGE WALK

NECKINGER

LAW STREET

**THE
WATCH
HOUSE**

4

SOUTHWARK

TABARD STREET

GRANGE

GRANGE

WALK

ROAD

SPA ROAD

⌂
N

0   200 m

TOWER BRIDGE ROAD

A

B

C

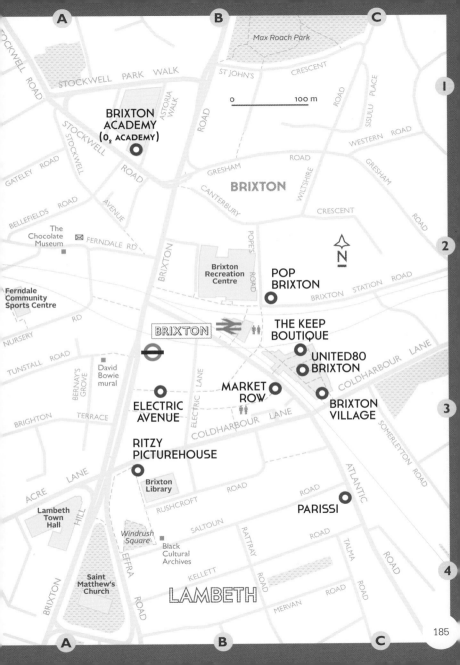

A
B
C

1

Max Roach Park

ST JOHN'S   CRESCENT

STOCKWELL ROAD

STOCKWELL PARK WALK

ASTORIA WALK

ROAD

SISULU PLACE

ROAD

WESTERN ROAD

GRESHAM ROAD

0   100 m

BRIXTON ACADEMY
(O₂ ACADEMY)

STOCKWELL ROAD

GATELEY ROAD

AVENUE

BELLEFIELDS ROAD

GRESHAM ROAD

BRIXTON

CANTERBURY

WILTSHIRE ROAD

CRESCENT

GRESHAM ROAD

2

The Chocolate Museum   ✉ FERNDALE RD

BRIXTON ROAD

POPES ROAD

Brixton Recreation Centre

POP BRIXTON

Ferndale Community Sports Centre

RD

NURSERY

BRIXTON

BRIXTON STATION ROAD

COLDHARBOUR LANE

TUNSTALL ROAD

BERNAY'S GROVE

David Bowie mural

THE KEEP BOUTIQUE

UNITED80 BRIXTON

ELECTRIC AVENUE

ELECTRIC LANE

MARKET ROW

BRIXTON VILLAGE

SOMERLEYTON ROAD

3

BRIGHTON TERRACE

COLDHARBOUR LANE

RITZY PICTUREHOUSE

Brixton Library

ROAD

ROAD

ATLANTIC

ACRE LANE

HILL

RUSHCROFT

PARISSI

Lambeth Town Hall

EFFRA ROAD

Windrush Square

Black Cultural Archives

SALTOUN

RATTRAY ROAD

ROAD

TALMA ROAD

ROAD

4

Saint Matthew's Church

BRIXTON

KELLETT ROAD

LAMBETH

MERVAN ROAD

ROAD

A
B
C

INDEX

ABOUT THE AUTHOR

Award-winning writer, journalist and author Penny Watson has lived in London twice over the past two decades. She married Philip King, an Englishman with a fittingly regal name, and has adopted his family during summer vacations ever since. Penny has travelled the world, written feature articles for countless magazines, newspapers and blogs, and researched a number of guidebooks including *Hong Kong Precincts*. She is currently working on three upcoming titles for Hardie Grant Travel: *Slow Travel – A Movement*, *Hong Kong Pocket Precincts* and *Ultimate Campsites: Australia*. She is a member of both the British Guild of Travel Writers and Australian Society of Travel Writers. She currently resides in Melbourne with Philip and her two children, Digby and Etienne.

ACKNOWLEDGEMENTS

Big thanks to everyone at Hardie Grant for publishing my second book. And especially to Melissa Kayser, Megan Cuthbert and Alice Barker for their editing skills and faith in my ability to get the job done. And to Michelle Mackintosh and Megan Ellis for making my words and pics look so enticing and evocative on the page.

The UK research trip wouldn't have happened without my wonderful and generous English in-laws Eddie and Denny who assisted in so many ways – good nosh, afternoon aperitives, grandparenting, the list goes on. That new toaster and kettle will never repay the debt of gratitude.

To my UK sisters and bros Lib and Jim, and Sarah and Christoph for their Plumtree and Wargrave hospitality; and good taste when it comes to homemade woodfired pizzas, underground bars and backyard soirees. And to their children, Tom, Will, Emily and new-to-the gang Felix, who are always so loving and giving to their Aussie cousins.

And I'm ever grateful to my beautiful husband Philip and children, Digby and Etienne, for always being enthusiastic and adventurous travellers whenever my work calls for it, and some. You never let me down. I love you … to the UK and back.

PHOTO CREDITS

Published in 2019 by Hardie Grant Travel,
a division of Hardie Grant Publishing

Hardie Grant Travel (Melbourne)
Building 1, 658 Church Street
Richmond, Victoria 3121

Hardie Grant Travel (Sydney)
Level 7, 45 Jones Street
Ultimo, NSW 2007

www.hardiegrant.com/au/travel

The maps in this publication incorporate data from
© OpenStreetMap contributors

OpenStreetMap is made available under the Open
Data Commons Open Database License (ODbL) by
the OpenStreetMap Foundation (OSMF): http://
opendatacommons.org/licenses/odbl/1.0.

Any rights in individual contents of the database are
licensed under the Database Contents License:
http://opendatacommons.org/licenses/dbcl/1.0/

Data extracts via Geofabrik GmbH https://www.
geofabrik.de

Contains National Statistics data © Crown copyright
and database right [2015]

Contains Ordnance Survey data © Crown copyright
and database right [2015]

The roundel and other transport symbols used on
maps © Transport for London

A catalogue record for this
book is available from the
National Library of Australia

London Pocket Precincts
ISBN 9781741176322

10 9 8 7 6 5 4 3 2 1

Publisher
Melissa Kayser

Senior editor
Megan Cuthbert

Project editor
Alice Barker

Proofreader
Helena Holmgren

Cartographer
Emily Maffei

Design
Michelle Mackintosh

Typesetting
Megan Ellis

Index
Max McMaster

Prepress
Megan Ellis and Splitting Image Colour Studio

Printed and bound in China by LEO Paper Group

Disclaimer: While every care is taken to ensure
the accuracy of the data within this product, the
owners of the data (including the state, territory
and Commonwealth governments of Australia) do
not make any representations or warranties about
its accuracy, reliability, completeness or suitability
for any particular purpose and, to the extent
permitted by law, the owners of the data disclaim
all responsibility and all liability (including without
limitation, liability in negligence) for all expenses,
losses, damages (including indirect or consequential
damages) and costs which might be incurred as a
result of the data being inaccurate or incomplete in
any way and for any reason.

Publisher's Disclaimers: The publisher cannot
accept responsibility for any errors or omissions.
The representation on the maps of any road or
track is not necessarily evidence of public right of
way. The publisher cannot be held responsible for
any injury, loss or damage incurred during travel.
It is vital to research any proposed trip thoroughly
and seek the advice of relevant state and travel
organisations before you leave.

Publisher's Note: Every effort has been made
to ensure that the information in this book is
accurate at the time of going to press. The publisher
welcomes information and suggestions for correction
or improvement.